HOW RELIGION EFFECTS CHILD DEVELOPMENT
CHILD DEVELOPMENT
and EDUCATION:
My Academic Freedom

Brandi Jo Searcy Atkins

WESTBOW
PRESS®
A DIVISION OF THOMAS NELSON
& ZONDERVAN

This book is a work of non-fiction. Unless otherwise noted, the author and the publisher make no explicit guarantees as to the accuracy of the information contained in this book and in some cases, names of people and places have been altered to protect their privacy.

WestBow Press books may be ordered through booksellers or by contacting:

WestBow Press
A Division of Thomas Nelson & Zondervan
1663 Liberty Drive
Bloomington, IN 47403
www.westbowpress.com
844-714-3454

Because of the dynamic nature of the Internet, any web addresses or links contained in this book may have changed since publication and may no longer be valid. The views expressed in this work are solely those of the author and do not necessarily reflect the views of the publisher, and the publisher hereby disclaims any responsibility for them.

Scripture quotations marked (NIV) are taken from the Holy Bible, NEW INTERNATIONAL VERSION®, NIV® Copyright © 1973, 1978, 1984, 2011 by Biblica, Inc.® Used by permission. All rights reserved worldwide.

Scripture quotations marked (ESV) are from the ESV® Bible (The Holy Bible, English Standard Version®), copyright © 2001 by Crossway, a publishing ministry of Good News Publishers. Used by permission. All rights reserved.

Scripture quotations marked (NKJV) are taken from the NEW KING JAMES VERSION (NKJV): Scripture taken from the NEW KING JAMES VERSION ®. Copyright© 1982 by Thomas Nelson, Inc. Used by permission. All rights reserved.

Scripture quotations marked (NLT) are taken from the Holy Bible, New Living Translation, copyright © 1996, 2004, 2015 by Tyndale House Foundation. Used by permission of Tyndale House Publishers, Carol Stream, Illinois 60188, USA. All rights reserved.

ISBN: 979-8-3850-4036-0 (sc)
ISBN: 979-8-3850-4037-7 (e)

Library of Congress Control Number: 2024926607

Print information available on the last page.

WestBow Press rev. date: 01/15/2025

CONTENTS

OPENING PRAYER

"O Lord, I give my life to You. I trust in You, my God! Do not let me be disgraced, or let my enemies rejoice in my defeat. No one who trusts in You will ever be disgraced, but disgrace comes to those who try to deceive others. Show me the right path, O Lord; point out the road for me to follow. Lead me by Your truth and teach me, for you are the God that saves me. All day long I put my hope in You. Remember, O lord, your compassion and unfailing love, which You have shown from long ages past. Do not Remember the rebellious sins of my youth. Remember me in the light of Your unfailing love, for You are merciful, O Lord." (Psalm 25: 1-7 David NLT)

ABOUT ME

"Who I am?" I enjoy walking on the treadmill spending time with God during my workout in prayer and reading his word. In my spare time my favorite thing to do is putting photo albums together and looking at memories. I love being in my jammies and cleaning house. I'm kind of like Monica on friends, everything needs to be neat and organized. But I am also like Kitty Forman from that 70's show as I always like having a house full of kids. I do not like to cook. I boil and microwave and my kids have had way more peanut butter sandwiches for dinner than I care to admit. My husband and I have been married for 25 years. I was planning my wedding my senior year of high school. I have two amazing, fun, loving boys. My parents were middle class and divorced when I was fourteen. I have a brother four years younger than me that I love very much.

My educational career started when I was 25 years old. The year was 2005 and I was still working on my undergrad course work. I began working as a Special Day Care aide for a local school district. I was there until 2008, during this time I resigned because I was pregnant and wanted to finish school. By the time our baby was born I had finished my BA degree in Liberal studies and entered the teaching credential program. In 2010 I began subbing for various school districts and worked with autistic children doing Applied Behavioral Analysis. In 2012, my second baby boy was on his way and by the time he was born I had one semester left to complete my Masters in Early Childhood Education. Even in my early college years I knew I wanted to be a college professor. I did not expect it to happen as quickly as it did. I was teaching a kindergarten class at a Catholic School in 2017 when I applied to a college to be an Adjunct Child Development Instructor. I went on the interview and got the job. That position also led to working at another position as an instructor at a different college. Each job has led to experiences and lessons. Some doors closed so others could open. I do feel that being a college instructor was my dream job. I feel the college world needs someone like me who is bold in their faith and not compromise faith for career. In the 6 years I have worked as a college instructor I have made mistakes and have learned and improved. Even professors who have worked for 40 years make mistakes and continue to learn and grow. I hope you learn from this book and come closer to God because of it.

Although I'm a teacher, I feel my first responsibility is raising my children. My main calling is teaching my children a firm foundation of faith, help them with their academics, and being present in their lives. Romans 12:4-8 New International Version: "For just as each of us has one body with many members, and these members do not all have the same function, so in Christ we, though many, form one body, and each member belongs to all the others. We have different gifts, according to the grace given to each of us. If your gift is prophesying, then prophesy in accordance with your faith; if it is serving, then serve; if it is teaching, then teach; if it is to encourage, then give encouragement; if it is giving, then give generously; if it is to lead, do it diligently; if it is to show mercy, do it cheerfully." I love doing daily devotions and prayer with my boys. I try to live a Christ like way through my actions; in the way I serve, give, teach, and encourage. My boys are rambunctious, loud, fun, and they love God. My relationship with God grew stronger after having kids. My oldest son was always asking Bible-based questions that I didn't have the answers to, and so I dug deeper to find them. He is currently a Junior in high school and wants to be a pastor. My youngest is funny, always makes me laugh, and is such a lovable sweet kid. He wants to be an engineer. God ordained the family before he ordained the church, so I make teaching my children a firm foundation of biblical truth a priority in our household. If we don't transmit our knowledge of God to the next generation, it will be lost. God uses the family unit to transmit His knowledge from one generation to the next and be "salt" and "light" to the world. In the Bible, salt and light are metaphors used by Jesus in Matthew 5:13-16. Salt is used to symbolize the ability to preserve or enhance, so Christians are called to preserve the moral values and live righteously. Light represents the truth and goodness, so Christians are called to shine their faith by demonstrating positive actions and character. Wouldn't it be wonderful to leave behind an amazing example of godliness for your children and grandchildren. If the family can be destroyed, the Christian fabric in society will ultimately unravel. Being a wife and a mom is the most important job I have. If you succeed everywhere else but your home, you are a failure. Are you raising your children to give glory to God? Only you can make parenting the priority it needs to be!

I had a calling to write and just started writing. I had some issues arising at my job and this book was therapeutic for me to write. My purpose for writing this book was my way to prove to college students and parents that Religion is extremely important in Child Development and Education. It is right up there with Safety and Nutrition. Did you know that Religion/faith/Bible/God is talked about in various child development text books? I'm only bringing out topics that is already in our curriculum. I have found such an intolerance to anything Religious based amongst college students and often even the staff. Adjuncts/part time college professors don't have academic freedom-at least not at the college I work at. Academic Freedom is a professional right that protects teachers, students and academic institutions from interference when pursing knowledge. It allows scholars, researchers, and educators to engage in teaching and scholarship without fear of censorship or retribution. This includes the freedom to raise difficult subjects in a classroom discussion and publish a controversial research paper. I could see how academic freedom can be taken to far with religion and politics. That being said those that can't express their academic freedom will find legal means to do so-Hence the book I'm writing. In this book I discuss all the ways religion is brought up in the text book, how it relates to children, bible scriptures that go along with the topic, the history of Christianity in Colleges, and validity of the Bible.

INFANTICIDE/ABORTION AND WHY WE PROTECT BABIES

A dults instinctively protect and cherish infants. This is essential in the survival of our species. But humans do not protect every baby. They might kill newborns that are not their own. In my Child Development Theories class in the 2nd chapter where we talk about Theories it discusses infanticide and references Jesus and Moses. It states in <u>The Developing Person Through Childhood and Adolescence 12th edition</u>, "The Christian Bible chronicles several examples, including two in the story of Moses and one in the birth of Jesus" (Berger). In the story of Moses, the Pharaoh wanted to depopulate the Israelites so that they would not try to overthrow him. He ordered the Egyptians to kill every newborn baby boy throwing them into the Red Sea. Moses' mother puts Moses into a basket and sends him into the water in the hopes he will be saved. He was. Ironically the Pharaoh's daughter raised him as her own. Jesus also escaped a time of Infanticide. King Herod found out that a King was born and ordered that all babies be killed. Joseph, Mary, and Jesus fled to Egypt to prevent Jesus from being killed.

According to the Child Development text book, <u>Understanding Child Abuse and Neglect</u> by Cynthia Crosson-Tower, In Chapter 1 it states, "Infanticide has occurred since early times. The Bible cites Abraham's intention to sacrifice his son, Isaac, to God. In early Rome, the father was given complete power to kill, abandon, or even sell his child. In Greek legend, Oedipus was doomed to death until he was rescued by a family retainer. In Hawaii, China, and Japan, many female and disabled children were killed to maintain a strong race without overpopulation. Infanticide was practiced for many reasons. Like the Hawaiians, Chinese, and Japanese, some cultures saw the practice of infanticide as a means of controlling and regulating the population so that society's resources could be expended on the strongest and most valued. As in the case of Abraham, babies were offered to appease Gods and infanticide was in some ways associated with religious beliefs. Attempts to limit family size or ensure financial security were also used as rationales for killing children (DeMause, 1998)."

Parents sometimes abandon newborns or while pregnant, drink, smoke, and do drugs. Biology as well as cultures favors traits that promote survival of the next generation. This explains some ancient practices that we now condemn such as letting a newborn die because it was a girl, or a twin, or a burden on the family in some other way. We live in a world where abortion is glorified, funded, and not seen as murder. I am a Child development college professor and in our child development textbook it addresses the issue as to when life begins. I presented an informal anonymous poll of when life begins and here is what I got:

> 1 student wrote that life begins at conception
>
> 7 wrote when the brain develops
>
> 12 wrote when there is a heartbeat
>
> 1 wrote outside the womb when baby can breathe air.

According to The Scientific Consensus on When a Human's Life Begins, "biologists from 1,058 academic institutions around the world assessed survey items on when a human's life begins and, overall, 96% (5337 out of 5577) affirmed the fertilization view."

Pro-life-The pro-life position is that life begins at fertilization, and that all human life is precious and made in the image of God.

Pro-Choice-The pro-choice position is that it is the woman's right to choose whether to have an abortion, because an unborn child is considered to be a part of the woman's' body. Under tis definition, the unborn child is not considered to be fully human.

Life begins at conception and the baby should be protected! All the genetic information to make an individual is present at fertilization, so right from the start a fertilized human egg cell is totally human. There is no biological basis for drawing any other line for when we become human every human is fully human from fertilization to the end of life. Abortion is the killing of an unborn child in his or her mother's womb. From both a biblical and scientific perspective, life begins at the moment of fertilization. Since abortion destroys a human being who is fearfully and wonderfully made in God's image, it is murder. "Before I formed you in the womb I knew you, before you were born, I set you apart" Jeremiah 1:5 NIV. The Lord is giving several pieces of information to the prophet. First, God says that He knew Jeremiah when he was in the womb. Second, He makes clear that He knew Jeremiah even before He was formed in the womb. Third, He tells Jeremiah that his growth in the womb was as a result of being "formed" by God Himself. It is a direct act of formation by God. Jeremiah 18 is the well-known chapter that talks about the potter and the clay. A similar image is being used of an unborn child in Jeremiah 1:5 where Jeremiah is a person-fully human.

College faculty is overwhelmingly pro-choice, and it rubs off on the students. "Fully 99 percent of Ivy League professors oppose a legal ban on abortion." (Shapiro). "Professor Peter Singer of Princeton University advocates the killing of disabled newborns." (Shapiro). "Professors are willing to go out on a limb to kill babies. Many professors even support the gruesome D&E (dilation and evacuation) a D&X procedure (dilation and extraction). A D&E is a late-term abortion wherein the doctor crushes the baby's skull in the uterus with forceps, then dismember the baby and extracts it. A D&X is also a late-term abortion, but in this one, a doctor pulls the baby through the birth canal by its feet, then cuts a hole in its skull and sucks its brains, afterward removing the corpse. To ban D&X is cruel, claims professor Susan Frelich Appleton of Washinton University in St. Louis." (Shapiro). For these 99 percent college professors' human life is not divine, and man should be able to take life away however they want to. Without a higher authority to answer to. Life belongs only to the one who possess it, and he or she can decide to end it through abortion, suicide, or euthanasia.

GOD GIVES LIFE, AND GOD TAKES IT AWAY. It is not up to the individual to decide when he should die. One might argue the life of the mother is at stake while giving birth and it is unfortunate that such very rare events happened "about 0.004 percent of all cases involve the possible death of the mother." (Ken Ham-The New Answers Book 3). I find it jaw dropping to me that academic freedom allows Professors the right to push their pro-choice agenda, but if I discuss infanticide in reference to Moses and Jesus as already discussed in the child development textbook that the school told me to teach from than I'm being told that I am not addressing student learning outcomes and should not be discussing religion in the classroom. Things that make you go HMMMM.

Not many organizations achieve the impact that planned parenthood has had on Western culture. At its root is an evolutionary philosophy taken that concludes that man is merely an animal in the process of evolving to his ultimate potential. Our right to life, ordained by the God of the universe, is at the core of a just society. It demands the leadership of the church, as we strive to uphold life as the Life-giver meant us to. The abortion debate is far more than a mere political issue. It is a sin issue.

Margaret Sanger, founder of planned parenthood, promoted birth control as a means of controlling the 'unfit' in society. Sanger stated: "The emergency problem of segregation and sterilization must be faced immediately. Every feeble-minded girl or woman of the hereditary type, especially of the intellectually disabled class, should be segregated during the reproductive period. Otherwise, she is almost certain to bear imbecile children, who in turn are just as certain to breed other defectives...Moreover, when we realize that each feeble-minded person is a potential source of an endless progeny of defect, we prefer the policy of immediate sterilization, of making sure that parenthood is absolutely prohibited to the feeble-minded." (Ken Ham-The New Answers book 3). "Her magazine, The Birth Control Review, contained many articles authored by leading eugenicists of her day. Sanger openly endorsed the concepts and methods of race purification carried out by the Nazis. Sanger believed sex was an evolutionary force that should not be prohibited because of its ability to created genius. In 1942, the American Birth Control League became the Planned Parenthood Federation of America (PPFA)." (Ken Ham-The New Answers Book 3).

According to the Book The New Answers Book 4 by Ken Ham. Here are some numbers of aborted children.

China estimates since 1971-2006: 300,000,000

USSR estimates from 1954-1991: 280,000,000

US estimates 1928-2007: 26,000,000

France estimates 1936-2006: 5,749,731

United Kingdom estimates 1958-2006: 6,090,738

Germany Estimates 1968-2007: 3, 699,624

THE GRAND ESTIMATE OF ABORTED CHILDREN ARE 621,500,000 and this excludes many other countries

To put that number in perspective here are some numbers lost in war. This information is also found in Ken Ham book The New Answers book 4 with a detailed reference list where Ken Ham got his information from as well. This is found on page 55 and 56 of his book and it speaks about the influence evolution has had on these wars.

Pre-Hitler Germany/Hitler and the Nazis

WWI: 8,500,000 WWII: 70,000,00 Holocaust: 17,000,000? (estimates range from 7 to 26 million) TOTAL ESTIMATE 95,000,000

Leon Trotsky and Vladimir Lenin Bolshevik revolution and Russian Civil War: 15,000,000

Joseph Stalin 20,000,000

Mao Zedong 14,000,000–20,000,000- MEDIAN ESTIMATE: 17,000,000

Korean War ~2,500,000?

Pol Pot (Saloth Sar) 750,000–1,700,000-MEDIAN ESTIMATE: 1,225,000

It is mind blowing to me that the total number of all these wars does not add up to the number of aborted children. This is excoriatingly painful to see.

Here are some other statistical analyses on abortion:

https://www.pewresearch.org/religion/religious-landscape-study/christians/christian/views-about-abortion/

https://www.hli.org/resources/planned-parenthood-abortion-statistics/

Planned parenthoods website only has one article on parenthood!!

When we start with the truth of God's Word, we see that eugenics and the ideas promoted by Planned Parenthood do not align with the Bible. The Bible shows that God considers all people equal. This is shown in Galatians 3:28 and Acts 17:26. The Bible shows that life is precious to God. The Bible shows the importance of caring for the needy as shown in Exodus 22:21-23 and Matthew 25:34-36.

Life is precious no matter how short or how impaired that life may be. Contrary to the ideas supported by eugenics and Planned Parenthood, all human life has value because it comes for the Life Giver! "Children are a gift from the Lord; they are a reward from him" (Psalm 127:3 New Living Translation). God remains faithful to his children and that includes you and me. At the same time, he desires his children to be faithful to him by obeying his word.

Psalm 139:13-16 New King James Version "For you formed my inward parts; You covered me in my mother's womb, I will praise You, for I am fearfully and wonderfully made; Marvelous are Your works, And that my soul knows very well. My frame was not hidden from you, When I was made in secret, And skillfully wrought in the lowest parts of the earth. Your eyes saw my substance, being yet unformed. And in Your book they all were written, The days fashioned for me, When as yet there were none of them."

This passage refers to the formation of flesh (covering), internal organs (inward parts), and bones (frame). None of these developments were hidden from God Though they were "secret" from people, indicating that we cannot directly see the formation of the unborn. The concept of the "lowest parts of the earth" is a euphemism for the female reproductive system. Even in this unborn, the baby is human, as God has already determined "the days fashioned" for the baby. "Viewing the evidence that shows that unborn babies can react to external stimuli, such as light and sound, is a further confirmation of their unique life apart from the mother." (Ken Ham The New Answers Book 3).

MORALITY AND CHILD DEVELOPMENT FROM A CHRISTIAN STAND POINT

Kohlberg's theory of moral development is a theory that focuses on how children develop morality and moral reasoning. This is in many child development text books. Kohlberg's theory suggests that moral development occurs in a series of six stages and that moral logic is primarily focused on seeking and maintaining justice. Moral development is the process by which people develop the distinction between right and wrong (morality) and engage in reasoning between the two (moral reasoning). Understanding Kohlberg's theory of moral development is important in that it can help parents guide their children as they develop their moral character. Teachers and other educators can also apply Kohlberg's theory in the classroom, providing additional moral guidance. A kindergarten teacher could help enhance moral development by setting clear rules for the classroom, and the consequences for violating them. This helps kids at stage one of moral development which is on punishment and obedience. A question I would pose to my college students is where do our morals come from? Most students often answer by saying our morals are passed down from our parents.

For Christians the fixed point of morality of right and wrong leads to God. If I gave an exam and a student cheated then I would point out that it was wrong to cheat. What bases do I have to say that cheating is morally wrong. Without a God there is no reason to be moral. There is no standard to what moral behavior is. If God does not exist than everything is permissible and pointless.

Lying, cheating, murder, stealing would have no consequences. Anyone who believes in an excuse for rape is evil. Anyone who believes in killing disabled children is evil. Anyone who flies planes into buildings with the intent of killing civilians is evil. "When professor Orlando Patterson of Harvard University was interviewed on NewsHour with Jim Lehrer regarding President Bill Clinton's perjury, he said, 'I think it's important to emphasize the fact that there are no absolutes in our moral precepts...Perjury in not an absolute. You don't have absolute rules here.' Wow. Perjury is okay because there are no absolutes. And if you don't agree, you're a fascist." (Shapiro). The assault on absolute morality is the basis for every brainwashing scheme of the left. We understand it's never morally right to lie, steal, or kill for the fun of it. We recognize culture itself cannot be the source of moral law, and there is instead a law about laws transcending all of us. All moral laws come from moral lawmakers. If there exists even one transcendent moral law that it's never morally right to kill someone for the fun of it then there must be a transcendent moral source. "In addition to this, Darwinian evolution, cannot produce truly objective morality. Objective morality must be rooted in something bigger than the evolutionary devolvement of any one species." (Wallace-Cold case Christianity)

"The problem is that evolutionists have no logical reason to believe in right and wrong within their own worldview. Right and wrong are Christian concepts that go back to Genesis. By attempting to be moral, therefore, the evolutionist is being irrational; for he must borrow biblical concepts that are contrary to his worldview. All things belong to God (Psalm 24:1) and thus, God has the right to make the rules. So, an absolute moral code makes sense in a biblical creation worldview. But if the Bible were not true, if human beings were merely the outworking of millions of years of mindless chemical processes, then why should we hold to a universal code of behavior? Could there really be such concepts as right and wrong if evolution were true?" (Ken Ham-How do we know the Bible is True? P. 167 and 168). If everyone can create his or her own morality, then no one could argue that what other people do is wrong, since other people can also invent their own personal moral code. Hitler convinced most of his people that his actions were right, but that doesn't make them right. To love and obey the God who has created and saved us should be our primary focus (Mark 12:30; Ecclesiastes 12:13). We should treat others with love and respect Matthew 7:12; Mark 12:31). If we are just chemical accidents then why should we care about anyone at all. Concern about others does not make sense in an evolutionary point of view. Evolutionist are inconsistent. If an evolutionist calls you a liar for teaching children about creation, then from their worldview, we should be able to lie. They borrow morality from the Bible. For morality to be meaningful, biblical creation must be true. We have inherited a sin nature from Adam who rebelled against God in the Garden of Eden. John 3:19 indicates that people would rather remain in spiritual darkness than have their evil deeds exposed. The solution to sin is confession and repentance (1 John 1:9; Luke 5:32). Christ is faithful to forgive anyone who calls on His name (Romans 10:13).

If you are an evolutionist your behavior and decisions will be much different than those who are Christian. Let's take drinking alcohol as an example. You've had a rough work week and on Friday you lose your job. You decide to get drunk as millions of Americans often do. You drive drunk. Wander into the other lane hitting a car and killing a family. Getting drunk is a perfectly acceptable behavior from an evolutionist point of view because there is no standard of right or wrong and taking another person's life really isn't all that bad. You don't believe me. Look at abortion statistics. Since God's word commands us to not get drunk, then to break the rule is sinful. Getting drunk is unacceptable to Christians. If people had a biblical worldview, then the amount of drunk driving would be drastically reduced. People think that believing in evolution is no big deal, but it leads to destructive behavior. People have abandoned the faith of their forefathers have embraced the doctrines of evolution with its atheism. We have become a "me, me, me" society where we want our self-desires fulfilled. This is a total contrast to what Christianity teaches. We are to give glory to God, not ourselves and enjoy Him forever. People left to do what seems right in their own eyes will end up doing what is wrong in God's eyes.

Here are some bible scriptures on morality:

Romans 13:8-10 ESV
Owe no one anything, except to love each other, for the one who loves another has fulfilled the law. For the commandments, "You shall not commit adultery, You shall not murder, You shall not steal, You shall not covet," and any other commandment, are summed up in this word: "You shall love your neighbor as yourself." Love does no wrong to a neighbor; therefore love is the fulfilling of the law.

Matthew 7:12 ESV
"So whatever you wish that others would do to you, do also to them, for this is the Law and the Prophets."

Mark 7:20-23 ESV
And he said, "What comes out of a person is what defiles him. For from within, out of the heart of man, come evil thoughts, sexual immorality, theft, murder, adultery, coveting, wickedness, deceit, sensuality, envy, slander, pride, foolishness. All these evil things come from within, and they defile a person."

1 Corinthians 6:9-11 ESV
Or do you not know that the unrighteous will not inherit the kingdom of God? Do not be deceived: neither the sexually immoral, nor idolaters, nor adulterers, nor men who practice homosexuality, nor thieves, nor the greedy, nor drunkards, nor revilers, nor swindlers will inherit the kingdom of God. And such were some of you. But you were washed, you were sanctified, you were justified in the name of the Lord Jesus Christ and by the Spirit of our God.

1 Corinthians 15:33 ESV
Do not be deceived: "Bad company ruins good morals."

Galatians 5:19-21 ESV

Now the works of the flesh are evident: sexual immorality, impurity, sensuality, idolatry, sorcery, enmity, strife, jealousy, fits of anger, rivalries, dissensions, divisions, envy, drunkenness, orgies, and things like these. I warn you, as I warned you before, that those who do such things will not inherit the kingdom of God.

WHY DOES NOT HAVING A FATHER IN THE HOME AFFECT A CHILD'S DEVELOPMENT AND WHAT DOES THAT HAVE TO DO WITH RELIGION?

As Will Smith put it in one of the most famous episodes of The Fresh Prince of Bel-Air, when his father has just walked out on him for the second time in his life:

> "Who needs him? He wasn't there to teach me how to shoot my first basket, but I learned. I got through my first date without him. I learned how to drive, learned how to shave, learned how to fight without him. I had 14 great birthdays without him...I didn't need him then, and I don't need him now...I'm going to get through college without him. I'm going to get a great job without him. I'm going to marry me a beautiful honey and have a whole bunch of kids, and I don't need him for any of that...How come he don't want me?"

"According to the U.S Census Bureau, 17.8 million children, nearly 1 in 4 live without a biological, step, or adoptive father in the home. That's enough children to fill New York City twice or Los Angeles four times over. Research shows that a fathers absence affects children in numerous ways, while a father's presence makes a positive difference in the live of both children and mothers." (U.S Census Bureau, 2023).

"On average, the single-parent structure functions less well for children because single parents have less income, time, and stability. Most single parents fill many roles-including wage earner this reduces time for emotional and academic support for children. If they are depressed that makes it worse" (Berger P. 352). In a Christian household the husband is the provider and the protector. The mother is the teacher and the nurturer. If the father is absent that leaves the mother to do all. I have also seen the opposite happen where the mother leaves all the responsibility to the father and the mother is absent in the home. Think in terms of this hierarchy: God is the head, Jesus is next, men are answerable to him, and woman are answerable to their husbands. The husband is going to have a lot more to answer to before God than a wife. I am less responsible than my husband is for how our family turns out. He is going to have to answer to God for every decision our family makes. So, if a father abandons his family or is destructive in any way he will have to answer to God on how his family turned out. This is the importance of the husband being the spiritual leader of the house hold, sadly this is not always the case.

"Never will I leave you; never will I forsake you." (Hebrews 13:5 NIV). That's the father that we all crave. That's the relationship that Jesus was born to have with you. That is the one that you've always been searching for. And once you've discovered it, it lasts forever. Jesus doesn't leave, disappoint, fail, hurt-or die. He is eternal.

HOW DOES DIVORCE AFFECT CHILD DEVELOPMENT AND WHAT ROLE DOES THE BIBLE PLAY

According to <u>The Developing Person Through Childhood and Adolescence 12<u>th</u> edition</u> it states that, "A study of 3,923 adult woman in the United States found that those who voluntarily had sex before age 16 were more likely to divorce later on, whether or not they become pregnant or later married their first sexual experience were also more likely to later experience divorce" (Paik, 2011, P.477). "In the United States, divorced, single-parent families were unusual in the 1960's, more common in the 1980's and 1990s, and again are less common in the twenty-first century. Children were more likely to suffer from divorce when divorce was rare. On average, however, children growing up in non-nuclear families have more emotional and academic problems than when both parents live in the same home as the child. The United States has more single parents than other developed nations, yet almost two-thirds of all U.S. school-age children live with two parents, most often their biological parents, and some of those children have emotional or academic problems as well... On average, nuclear families function best; children living with two married parents tend to learn more in school with fewer psychological problems" (Berger P.347).

Jesus confirmed his understanding of marriage when he was asked about divorce by the Pharisees. This is recorded in Mark 10:1-12 and Mathew 19:1-12. Jesus said that divorce was only allowed because of the hardness of the hearts of man. God intended, from the beginning, for marriages to consist of one man and one woman for the duration of their lives. Divorce and polygamy were regulated in the laws given to Moses, but polygamy was recorded long before then. Just because the Bible records polygamous relationships does not mean that God approves of such things. This is shown in 1 Timothy 3:2 and 12 and Titus 1:6. A marriage is a holy Union, God ordained and Christ centered. Most people don't go into a wedding ceremony as it being any of that. When you put God at the center of your marriage and wedding ceremony you are less likely to be abusive, commit adultery, to have a drug and alcohol problem. In the Bible there is a story of a husband whose wife is a prostitute and God said stay with her anyway. This is because her Salvation is more important than your feelings. This story you will find in the book of Hosea. This parallels Gods love for us as God is our Groom and we are his bride. God is a faithful husband. The broken marriage and children are a prophetic symbol of Gods relationship to Israel. Israel has rebelled and God will bring severe consequences. But Gods Love and Mercy are more powerful than Israels sin. God wants his people to know him and experience his love. The most striking thing about Hosea is his willingness to forgive the unworthy Gomer, even at great personal cost. In the same way, God offered forgiveness to the equally unworthy Israel. It is one thing to forgive someone who has asked for your forgiveness. It is something altogether Christlike to forgive someone who has offended you in the past and continues to do so proudly. Continue to pray for your wife/husband and be a light to her/him in the hopes that she/he will be reunited with having a relationship with God. Most divorces happen because people are flawed and out for their own selfish desires instead of following God's will and being obedient to him. The evidence of knowing God is obeying God. By obeying God, you will gain more than you can give. When you have a Christ centered marriage than your able to learn how to forgive and give grace and mercy. Commitment during conflicts produces character. Love in marriage grows and deepens when exercised through faith-stretching circumstances: sickness, unexpected job change, babies, extended family members, bills, times apart. In each case God is big enough to meet your need and wise enough to use even difficult times to deepen your commitment to him and to one another. Your commitment to God first then your spouse. The power of prayer is amazing. God's ability to change people is amazing. Do you pray for your spouse? Would a commitment to God change your relationship for the better? How would prayer change you? Ask God that whatever your circumstance may be that he uses it to strengthen your commitment to your spouse. PRAYER WORKS! I'VE SEEN IT!!

Matthew 5:32- Divorce in the Bible is only considered under the only exceptional circumstance of sexual immortality. If either spouse remarries a person not divorced under this rule, or if they have not been divorced because of immoral behavior, then they will have committed adultery. When you marry, you become one flesh, therefore, treating your spouse badly is like beating up on yourself! Pain and suffer are the obvious results for both partners (Genesis 2:24, Mark 10: 8-10). "However, each one of you also must love his wife as he loves himself, and the wife must respect her husband. (Ephesians 5:33 NIV). Wives, in the same way, submit yourselves to your own husbands so that, if any of them do not believe the word, they may be won over without words by the behavior of their wives" (1 Peter 3:1 New International Version).

It is important in a marriage to be equally yoked. Gods' preference is for a Christian to marry a Christian, this is an example of being evenly yoked. Often when you are unevenly yoked, say a Christian marrying an atheist then you most definitely will have problems in your marriage. 2 Corinthians 6:14 NIV states, "Do not be yoked together with unbelievers" in the living Bible translation it states, "Don't be teamed with those who do not love the Lord, for what do the people of God have in common with the people of sin? How can light live with darkness? Examine your relationship with non-Christians before they become too involved or permanent. Pulling together is impossible because they are marching two different drumbeats. If you take pride in yourself, your possessions, or your abilities this will only bring destruction. If you have Humility before God, before others, before yourself this will bring honor. Just as pride caused Lucifer to want to be greater than God (Isaiah 14:12-14), resulting in condemnation (1 Timothy 3:6). So, pride can ruin your life. Have humility before God and your spouse. Nothing is as hard to do gracefully as getting down off your high horse. Place your spouses needs above your own. Go out of your way to express a word of sincere appreciation. Remember Pride covers your owns sins, pride obscures the view of others, and pride hinders service for God! Are you marrying someone who loves the lord? Are you marrying someone with different beliefs than you such as a Mormon marrying a Catholic? How will your kids be raised? If you are not equally yoked in your marriage than your marriage will suffer and often lead to divorce. The husband is to be the head of the household spiritually. Wives are to be submissive to their husbands and trust their judgment. Do households today have submissive wives or husbands as their spiritual leaders?

My husband and I have been married for 25 years. I was planning my wedding my senior year of High School. Although over the years my relationship with God has gotten stronger, faith was important to me when I got married. I got married in a church, stayed abstinent 6 months before marriage, and our wedding bands has a cross on it to symbolize the importance of a Christ centered marriage. Throughout our 25 years of marriage, we struggled with porn addiction, concerns of infidelity, insecurities, health scares, and hurtful words to one another. I'm sure if I was to of married someone else, they would have left me and vice versa, but because our marriage is a holy union, God ordained, and Christ Centered-Divorce was never an option! Forgiveness, grace, mercy, and trust are all Christ centered attributes. I am not saying it was easy or that it didn't take time, but I am saying that God meant more to me than my husband. Following his will and not mine. Making my husband's salvation a priory over my hurt feelings. THIS IS A HARD PILL TO SWALLOW IN THE HEAT OF THE MOMENT! I cannot wrap my head around people who are Christians and get divorced. I begin to think if I was able to put God first in my marriage than why can't others. Then I got to thinking everyone's journey with God is different. Sometimes you must hit rock bottom, lose everything including your marriage, home, kids, job, and respect of others to turn to God. God does not promise you a life that will be easy. In fact, he guarantees that there will be hard times. It's the transformation/journey that's important. Affairs happen because you didn't put God first in your marriage. Abuse and addictions happen because you did not put God first in your marriage. You followed your own selfish desires. It takes two to get married and it takes two to get divorced. What part did you play in that divorce? Can you forgive yourself? Can you forgive your ex? Can you humble yourself and be happy for them now? Can you strive for Peace? If God was not first in your marriage, then, Can you turn to God now and say from this point on I will make God at the center of my relationships? What will happen if you don't? Can the same mistakes be repeated? God is your ultimate counselor he should be who you turn to for advice and healing. Be enlightened by Gods word and be bold and passionate in prayer for yourself and your spouse.

CHILD-REARING

WANTED- Energetic young couple for demanding assignment. Must have lots of patience, stamina, and optimism. Must be able to function well on four hours of sleep, must be able to diagnose illnesses, read the same book eighty-two times without appearing to be bored. Must be a skilled veterinarian, counselor, teacher, and taxi driver. Full time position, no paid vacations, salary won't change based on experience, you might lose your sanity. In case you have not guessed it. The position available is that of a parent. What greater challenge for a parent is there than to communicate God's timeless truth to a tender young life? God has a word of counsel just for you! This is in Deuteronomy 6:6-7-the key to passing faith is not lecturing or giving your child good books to read, but rather taking advantage of the teachable moments in the daily classroom of life: mealtime, playtime, bedtime-golden moments when little minds are more impressionable for God. Look for a teachable moment in your child's life today. Then seize it and use it for eternity. You'll be glad you did.

"Train up a child in the way he should go; even when he is old, he will not depart from it." (Proverbs 22:6 ESV). In my Child Development Ecology class this quote is in the first chapter. The book is titled Child, Family, School, Community Socialization and Support 10th Edition by Roberta M. Berns. So, we talk about what this quote means. Can parents do everything they are supposed to and their child stray from faith, if so, how does this happen? Since this class discusses nature verses nurture which is genes verses environment, I will ask the students what environmental influences occur for a child to led away from faith? Here we discuss peer influences, media, and entertainment. Can a child go through a phase where they turn away from their faith but, then return. If so, how does this happen? What environmental influences take place? How do godly parents end up with rebellious children? The parents' firsthand knowledge of God never became more than secondhand information to the children. Through oversight or neglect, the parents never challenged their children to discover how God could be real in their own lives. Each new generation must respond to him personally, and find him to be all they need for their needs. I have seen God work in my life so many times. As parents are you denying your children those same experiences. Are children resisting parents' effort to show you the reality of faith in God? Many parents give their children everything except themselves. What are you doing today to help your children accomplish great things for God tomorrow? Your example is not just one way to attract your children to Christ, it is the only way.

"Spare the rod, spoil the child" is a popular saying. This saying is not in the Bible, but in the Bible, it does talk about the Rod. "He who spares his rod hates his son, But he who loves him disciplines him promptly." (Proverbs 13:24 NKJV). In the child development textbook, The Developing Person through Childhood and Adolescence, 12th edition by Kathleen Stassen Berger there is an article on page 269 called, Spare the Rod? Attached is the article.

> "Opinions about spanking are influenced by past experiences and cultural norms. That makes it hard for opposing perspectives to be understood by people on the other side (Ferguson, 2013). Try to suspend your own assumptions as you read this.
>
> What might be right with spanking? Over the centuries, many parents have done it, so it has stood the test of time and has been a popular choice. Spanking is less common in the twenty first century than in the twentieth (Taillieu et al.,2014).

However, 85 percent of U.S. adolescents who were children at the end of the twentieth century recall being slapped or spanked by their mothers (Bender et al., 2007). In low-and middle-income nations, over a third of the mothers believe that physical punishment is essential to raise a child well (Deater-Deckard & Lansford, 2016).

Those who are pro-spanking need to explain why spanking correlates with later depression, low achievement, aggression, crime, and so on. They suggest that a third variable, not spanking itself, is the reason for that connection. One possible third variable is misbehavior: Perhaps disobedient children cause spanking, not vice versa. Such children may become delinquent, depressed, and so on not because they were spanked, but in spite of being spanked.

Noting problems with correlational research, one team explains, "Quite simply, parents do not need to use corrective actions when there are no problems to correct" (Larzelere & Cox, 2013, p.284).

Further, since parents who spank their children often have less education and money than other parents, low SES may be the underlying crucial variable. Perhaps spanking is a symptom of poverty and poor parenting skills. If that is true, to reduce the low achievement, aggression, and depression, we need to increase education and income, not to ban spanking (Ferguson, 2013).

Another pro-spanking response to the troubling research is to argue that researchers need to be careful in how they define corporal punishment. If a study does not distinguish between severe corporal punishment and milder, occasional spanking, then the data will show that spanking is harmful-but that conclusion reflects the harm of severe punishment (Larzelere et al., 2017).

Now the opposing perspective.

What might be wrong with spanking? One problem is adults' emotions. Angry spankers may become abusive. Children have been seriously injured and even killed by parents who use corporal punishment.

Another problem is the child's immature cognition. Parents assume that transgression is obvious, but children may think that the parents' anger, not the child's actions, caused spanking (Harkness et al., 2011). Most parents tell their children why they are being spanked, but when they are hit, children are less likely to listen or understand, much less learn.

Almost all of the research finds that children who are physically punished suffer overall (Grogan-Kaylo et al., 2018). Compared to children punished in other ways, they are more depressed, anti-social, and lonely. Many hates school and have few close friends. Emotional and social problems in adulthood are more common in people who were spanked as children—true for relatively mild spanking as well as for more severe spanking.

One reason for these correlations is that spanked children more often have angry, depressed, unloving parents. However even among children of warm and loving parents, spanked children tend to be more anxious, worried they will do something to lose their parents' affection (Lansford et al., 2014).

So, who is right? I know which perspective is mine. Most developmentalists believe that alternatives to spanking are better for children and a safeguard against abuses. I agree with that. The same study that found spanking common in developing nations also reported that 17 percent of the children experience severe violence that no developmentalist would condone (Bornstein et al., 2016). That alone is reason to stop.

I recognize that there are exceptions—spanked children who become happy and successful adults. For example, one study found that conservative evangelical parents spank their children more often than other parents, but if that spanking occurred only in early (not middle) childhood, the children did not develop low self-esteem and increased aggression (Ellison et al., 2011).

The authors of the study suggest that, since spanking was the norm in that group, spanked children did not feel unloved. Moreover, religious leaders told the parents never to spank in anger. As a result, some children may "view mild-to-moderate corporal punishment as legitimate, appropriate, and even an indicator of parental involvement, commitment, and concern (Ellison et al., 2011, P. 957).

Another study of conservative Christians found that many thought their faith condoned spanking. Only when they learned that the Bible opposed spanking) e.g., that "sparing the rod" refers to the guiding rod that shepherds use, which was never used to punish), and learned research on the long-term harm, did they change their minds (Perrin et al., 2017). Many then concluded that physical punishment in contrary to their belief in love and forgiveness.

A dynamic-systems, multicultural perceptive reminds me that everyone is influenced by background and context. I know that I am; so is every scientist; so are you. Probably my opinions are wrong about several developmental controversies that I explain in this text. I do not think this is one of them.

That concludes the article on Spare the Rod? Here are my thoughts on the article. I highlighted a part of the article for you to see that I found was taken out of context. As someone who has read the Bible several times makes me wonder what else this college text book could have that is taken out of context. Common sense would tell you that a rod was used to push sheep to guide them to go a certain way. Spanking is biblically okay in an extreme unsafe situation, a child is deliberately defiant and disobedient, or severely disrespectful. Spanking is NOT biblically okay when a child is being childish, impulsive, or had an accident. "Do not withhold discipline from a child; if you strike him with a rod, he will not die" (Proverbs 23:13 ESV). In other words, if one does not discipline a child, he or she will never learn obedience and good manners. "Whoever spares the rod hates his own, but he who loves him is diligent to discipline him" (Proverbs 13:24 ESV). "Folly is bound up in the heart of a child, but the rod of discipline drives it far from him" (Proverbs 22:15 ESV). The Bible does say to give discipline. Even fathers were to give their children the rod. To withhold it is considered unloving (Proverbs 13:24, 23:13). So, beating with a rod or more appropriately a branch is not harsh but required for discipline. Even the Apostle Paul reveals he was beaten with a rod 3 times (2 Corinthians 11:25), and he didn't die from it. In today culture of spankings was common in public schools until just a few decades ago. Only recently this has been deemed inappropriate.

Here is my take away as a Christian mother who is a Child Development Professor. Nothing good can come out of spanking your kids in anger as this could lead to abuse. It is important in the heat of the moment parents calm down first before spanking. Once calm you can explain to the child why they are getting spanked.

Afterwards always show love, so the child knows you still love them. It is not necessary to spank your child for every misbehavior. For example, with my kids I always spanked when a sin had occurred such as lying, stealing, disrespect to parents, cheating on a test, or getting sent to the principal's office. My kids always knew if you were in trouble at school, you were also in trouble at home. But other disciplinary actions also took place such as time outs, sentence writing, going to bed early, no desserts and as they got older no electronics. I tried to have the punishment fit the crime. For example, if they got a dessert without asking then they didn't get any dessert the rest of the day or the next day. If they were rough housing and a lightsaber went through a wall then they helped fixed the hole and did chores around the house at a price I set until I felt the damaged had been paid. I usually spanked with my hand until about 4th grade then it was a belt, and it was always 3 swats. Some kids' spankings are very effective for discipline. Others kids you could spank them repeatedly for the same incident and they'll still do it, in these cases it's best to find other ways to discipline that are more effective. By the time my kids were in Jr. High I no longer saw spanking as a way of discipline. Taking away electronics and keeping them away from their friends for a couple of days is much more effective. I do not enjoy disciplining my children. But there is something more painful to a parent than giving a spanking, and that is giving repeated spankings for the same offense. Discipline has only achieved its goal when it produces a change. Tears of remorse may show a changed heart, but unless followed by acts of repentance the discipline has failed to achieve its desired end. If spanking is to become a part of your parenting toolkit, it should be done with Love. Effective spanking involves responding in love, not reacting in fear-the fear that you've lost control of this child you are raising. Spanking outside of a loving relationship only produces angry kids. It is less painful to discipline a child than to weep over a spoiled youth. Children need love, especially when they do not deserve it. Although children need to learn instant obedience to their parents as we are called to give obedience to God. It is also important to explain convictions. For example, a father might say

"Do what your told" and a child might ask, "Why" and the father might say, "Because I said so." As parents you need to take the time to explain to your child. Your child will respect you more for it. Stike a balance between child discipline. Corporal punishment is biblical (Proverbs 23:13-14) but there should also be a balance. Proverbs 19:18 NLT says, "Discipline your children while there is hope. Otherwise, you will ruin their lives." Firm but gracious discipline should characterize the home. First time obedience is necessary. When you give a count down for them to do something by the time you count to five you are given them control to do things on their time not yours. You are giving them five more seconds for them to disobey. Delayed obedience is disobedience. I often hear from my own kids, "wait a minute mom, or I will do it after this game." Immediate obedience is important to practice with your kids as this will help them when they are older to have immediate obedience to God and say "Yes Lord, I will do whatever you need Lord," and with a happy heart.

The influence of parents on their children is strong. Children are born to mimic you and others. They are super observant. Do you hold the Christ like example you want your children to have? Make a list about some things you like and don't like about what you see in your spiritual life. If your children grow up to follow in your footsteps, will you be pleased where those footsteps lead? It's also important for your children to see you fail. Children need to hear how you disobeyed your heavenly father and how you felt his hand of discipline and how you learned from it and loved him even more because of it. Children will follow footsteps more easily than they will follow advice. Children learn best from example; the trouble is, they don't know a good example from a bad one? Your best investment in the future is a godly influence in the present. How are you seeking to influence the children in your life for God and for good? Does God agonize when he must bring painful consequences upon his children? Sometimes God must discipline parents as well as the children. A few biblical examples would be Moses who wasn't able to enter into the promised land due to his sin, David's child that died due to his affair and murder. Although God forgives, there are consequences to our sins. The husband who is the spiritual head of the household is the one who answers for how his family has turned out. Is your marriage a success? Are you trying to raise children that are an asset to God, the church, and society? Then don't overlook God in your family. You will have a God honoring home if you are diligent, hardworking, and have God in your home. Psalm 127, "Children are a gift from God; they are his reward." They are also a responsibility, for God wants the parents to launch them into life. Make time for God to be a part of your life; do family devotions, prayer, and discussions. Allow your children the opportunity to feel comfortable around you to tell you anything.

CHILD DEVELOPMENT IN REGARDS TO OBESITY AND BIBLICAL TRUTH

According to the child development textbook, <u>The Developing Person Through Childhood and Adolescence 12<u>th</u> Edition</u>:

> "Obesity correlates with poverty for many reasons. Families with little money or education are more likely to get less exercise, watch more TV, eat fewer vegetables, drink more sugary drinks, and buy more fast food (Cespedes et al., 2013)." "Children who grow up in food-insecure households learn to eat whenever food is available, becoming less attuned to hunger and the signals in their bodies. Consequently, as adults, they overeat when they are not hungry" (S.Hill et al., 2016). "In 2016, 14 percent of 2-to 5-year-olds, 18 percent of 6-to 11-year-olds, and 21 percent of 12-to 19-year old's in the United States were obese (Fryar et al., 2018). Childhood obesity is linked to childhood depression (Sutaria et al., 2019) as well as to lack of exercise and excess screen time, both of which make the problem worse."

According to the CDC, as of January 2024, "1 in 5 children and adolescents in the United States are obese, with the following percentage by age group: 2-5 years old 12.7%. 6-11 years old 20.7% and 12-19 years old 22.2%. You can see from the statistics from 2016 until current have gone up just a little bit.

As Christians we need to pray for the American church to set an example for unbelievers in the way we think about and treat our bodies. God's word provides more than enough motivation for taking steps to get healthy. We must glorify God in our body and in our spirit, which are His (1Corinthians 6:19-20). Our bodies belong to God, but he has bestowed their care on us as a stewardship responsibility to glorify God in our body as well as our spirit. (Luke 16:1-13). In a household that holds biblical truth as important, taking care of our bodies is done out of obedience to God. Eating healthy and exercising shows that I am using my body to glorify God. Other ways to not use my body to glorify God would be the following:

> Having an abortion would not be using my body to glorify God.
>
> Having sex before marriage would not be using my body to glorify God.
>
> Becoming a prostitute would not be using my body to glorify God.
>
> Using drugs would not be using my body to glorify God.
>
> Changing my gender would not be using my body to glorify God.
>
> Drinking alcohol for the purpose of getting drunk is not using my body to glorify God.

I work out 5 days a week. I drink a lot of water. I take vitamins. I do my best to eat healthy. God is trusting us to take care of our earthly bodies. This also means making sure that you get the right amount of sleep, so you have the energy to serve him throughout your day, being modest in clothing and the things that we say. We want to show God that we are taking care of HIS body! If you live in a house hold that holds biblical truth as important than I think that you would be less likely to have obese children weather you are a low-income family or not. That being said I know a lot of Christians who are obese and your salvation with Jesus Christ is NOT determined by how much you weigh. Jesus loves you.

CHILD DEVELOPMENT- RELIGIOUS, POLITICAL, RACIAL, AND SEXUAL IDENTITY

Religious Identity-There are four aspects of identity: religious, political, vocational, and sexual. According to the Child Development college textbook The Developing Person through Childhood and Adolescence 12th edition by Berger it states that, "Most adolescent question some aspects of their faith, but their religious identity is similar to that of their parents. The search for religious identity may be universal, as a study of youth in eight nations suggests (Bensorn et al., 2012). Most of the research has been on Christian youth in Western nations. However, a recent study in Japan reported that Buddhist adolescents also seek to establish their own religious beliefs and practices (Sugimura et al., 2019). Some become more devout. A Muslim girl might start to wear a headscarf; a Catholic boy might study for the priesthood; a Baptist teenager might join a Pentecostal youth group. Although becoming more devout than their parents is possible, the more common pattern is rebellion. Attendance at churches, temples, and mosques decreases when parents no longer enforce it. More common than either extreme is a moratorium that allows later achievement of religious identity. Adolescents question 'organized religion' because it seems to be a bundle of beliefs and rituals. They reexamine each part of the package, seeking their own way to be spiritual yet open" (Saroglou, 2012, Berger P.425).

My personal relationship with God grew stronger after having children. My oldest son constantly questioned How was the earth created? How were humans created? He questioned Bible stories

and would ask questions like Why would God destroy the earth
with a flood or use plaques? Finding the answers for him became
an overwhelming task. The questions never stopped and I wanted
to try to find the answers for him. Answers to Genesis series by
Ken Hamm helped us. My parents went to church occasionally and
my husband growing up never went to church. My husband and
I started going to church in our adolescent stage, but our parents
did not lead that example, we made that choice for ourselves. I can
see how our religious beliefs have impacted our children since my
oldest talks about wanting to be a minister and rebels not against us,
but the ideology of our society we live in. A new study published in
Social Psychological and Personality Science shows that the number
one predictive factor for an American child becoming an atheist is
growing up in a home with little religion or religious activity.

> "For children and teens especially, consistent
> Christian presence in their life can make a big impact
> towards them continuing to walk with Christ and in
> the church. This is the cultural context the research
> reveals. As we minister to families through children's
> ministry, youth ministry, VBS, and other activities,
> we can be assured that these moments of contact
> make a difference in their lives. Kids and teens want
> the same things adults do: people who accept them,
> people they can confide in, people they can rely on,
> people that can model a good, joyful life. They can
> either try to find someone like that through the latest
> social media celebrity, a teacher, coach, or family
> member who does not live like Jesus. Or they can
> find it in us, leaders and pastors who are living the
> discipleship journey with joy. At the end of the day,
> we know Christianity to be true based on the logical
> reasoning for the existence of God and the validity
> of the Bible and all that's within it. Atheists can
> claim higher intellect, but it's just not true. We're
> also remined of the powerful influence of consistent

trusted relationship in our upbringing, in the way we believe or not believe. Though we know God is the One opening hearts and minds to receive Him, we stay passionate on our part to partner with Him to reach the future generation with the hope of the gospel, mainly through our faithful presence in their lives" (Social Psychological and Personality Science).

Generations ago, parenting decisions were easier to make because it was assumed that one's main purpose in life was to serve God by being faithful and following the teachings of one's religion. Belief in a hierarchal order of status and obedience to authority were valued. Children were constantly exhorted to overcome their base natures in order to please God. This concept is still preached by some of the fundamentalist religious sects around the world.

In chapter 3 of the Child Development Ecology textbook <u>Child, Family, School, Community Socialization, and support 10th Edition</u> by Roberta M. Berns, it states that,

> "Religion is a 'unified system of beliefs and practices relative to sacred things, uniting into a single moral community all those who adhere to those beliefs and practices' (Durkheim, 1947, p.47)." "Religion is a macrosystem in that if influence patterns of gender roles, sexual behavior, marriage, divorce, birthrates, morals, attitudes, and child rearing. It also may affect one's dress, dietary habits, alcohol consumption, health cares, and social interactions, including ethics" (Gollnick & Chinn, 2012). "Religion influences socialization in that it has been one of the major influences on human thought and behavior throughout history. It has profoundly affected individuals' families, communities, and cultures. It has motivated people to have morally, philosophize about life's purpose, and speculate about an afterlife. It has stimulated techniques such as prayer,

ritual, and mediation, by which believers can find psychological comfort. It has been an inspiring force in architecture, art, music, politics, business, health care, social work, and education" (Fontana, 2003). "If the family subscribes to an organized religion, at birth children are often inducted into it via a public naming ceremony. The family's religious beliefs determine what is selected from the environment to transmit to the child. The family also interprets and evaluates what is transmitted. For example, Roman Catholics believe in strict obedience to authority and do not believe in divorce or birth control. Children from Roman Catholic families are brought up to obey their parents and the church. They are also reared to believe in the sanctity of marriage and to believe that sex is for producing children."

Here are some Bible scriptures to go along with the topic:

Genesis 1:27 English Standard Version (ESV) "So God created man in his own image, in the image of God he created him; male and female he created them."

2 Corinthians 5:17 ESV "Therefore, if anyone is in Christ, he is a new creation. The old has passed away; behold, the new has come."

1 Peter 2:9 ESV "But you are a chosen race, a royal priesthood, a holy nation, a people for his own possession, that you may proclaim the excellencies of him who called you out of darkness into his marvelous light."

Jeremiah 1:5 ESV "Before I formed you in the womb I knew you, and before you were born I consecrated you; I appointed you a prophet to the nations."

Galatians 2:20 ESV "I have been crucified with Christ. It is no longer I who live, but Christ who lives in me. And the life I now live in the flesh I live by faith in the Son of God, who loved me and gave himself for me."

Ephesians 2:10 ESV "For we are his workmanship, created in Christ Jesus for good works, which God prepared beforehand, that we should walk in them."

Jeremiah 29:11 ESV "For I know the plans I have for you, declares the Lord, plans for welfare and not for evil, to give you a future and a hope."

1 Corinthians 12:27 ESV "Now you are the body of Christ and individually members of it."

John 15:15 ESV "No longer do I call you servants, for the servant does not know what his master is doing; but I have called you friends, for all that I have heard from my Father I have made known to you."

1 Corinthians 6:19-20 ESV "Or do you not know that your body is a temple of the Holy Spirit within you, whom you have from God? You are not your own, for you were bought with a price. So glorify God in your body."

Political Identity-In chapter 3 of the child development ecology textbook <u>Child, Family, School, Community Socialization, and Support 10th Edition</u> by Roberta M. Berns, it states that "Not only does religion influence families and their socialization of children but it influences the community as well, in respect to values and behavior. The dominant religious group in the United States (Protestants) has undoubtedly influenced the political and economic foundation of our country (Weber, 1930). The Protestant ethic is a religiously derived value system that defines the ideal person as individualistic, thrifty, self-sacrificing, efficient in use of time, strong in personal responsibility, and committed to productivity. By following this value system, believers feel one can reach salvation. An example of the Protestant ethic's influence on politics is welfare reform-laws passed to require welfare recipients to work (be self-sufficient) after a certain amount of time receiving government assistance. Religious beliefs can affect communities when religious groups elect member to government in offices and school boards to influence policies such as abortion laws, school prayer, and science curriculum."

Political Identity is also discussed in the child development textbook The Developing Person through Childhood and Adolescence 12th edition. "Someone who identifies as a religious conservative may be troubled if they also identify as a gender nonbinary, or someone who identifies as African American may be troubled by assumptions about their politics..." (Berger, P. 429). Christians who believe and read the Bible often see this quote as troubling. If you are Christian then you believe that your physical body is not yours but God's. You use your body to give glory to God. You are obedient to his will and not your own. This means you cannot change your gender because you want to, or want to change what the ideology of marriage is. Salvation is not based on faith alone, but living the lifestyle that God would approve of. You have obedience to him BECAUSE of faith. You can go to church and say that you're a Christian, but that doesn't mean you have salvation. Salvation is the result of God's grace. Of course, we all fall short and sin, but when you're choosing to be born again you are choosing to leave behind a life of sin and living a Christ like life. If you are a Christian and you read the Bible then you also understand that we are all one race one blood. God did not create different races he created different cultures with different languages during the Tower of Babel. Race is a social construct. Although I see the conflict that an African American may have for voting for an African American man for the sole purpose of having a first Black president, but if their policies on abortion, marriage, or racism go against Biblical truth and you vote for him anyway, then are you idolizing man or God? Parents influence their children's political identity as well. Religion can influence who you are voting for politically. My husband and I are both passionate about politics and we can see that rub off on our children. Abortion, racism, LGBTQAI+ are sin issues not political ones. I won't vote for anyone who is pro-choice, supports the LGBTQAI+ community and encourages racism. From a Christians point of view, we are all one race one blood. In chapter four of Child, Family, School, Community Socialization and Support by Roberta M. Berns it states, "The political ideology of various religious and ethnic groups has influenced parenting practices through history, because traditionally the nation's head represented the major religious or ethnic group. Today, there are exceptions, especially in progressive countries where there is great religious or ethnic diversity" (Berns P. 126).

Here are some Bible scriptures that go along with the topic:

> Titus 3:1 ESV "Remind them to be submissive to rulers and authorities, to be obedient, to be ready for every good work,"

> 1 Timothy 2:1-2 ESV "First of all, then, I urge that supplications, prayers, intercessions, and thanksgivings be made for all people, for kings and all who are in high positions, that we may lead a peaceful and quiet life, godly and dignified in every way."

> Philippians 3:20 ESV "But our citizenship is in heaven, and from it we await a Savior, the Lord Jesus Christ,"

> Romans 13:1-7 ESV "Let every person be subject to the governing authorities. For there is no authority except from God, and those that exist have been instituted by God. Therefore whoever resists the

authorities resists what God has appointed, and those who resist will incur judgment. For rulers are not a terror to good conduct, but to bad. Would you have no fear of the one who is in authority? Then do what is good, and you will receive his approval, for he is God's servant for your good. But if you do wrong, be afraid, for he does not bear the sword in vain. For he is the servant of God, an avenger who carries out God's wrath on the wrongdoer. Therefore one must be in subjection, not only to avoid God's wrath but also for the sake of conscience. ..."

Acts 5:29 ESV "But Peter and the apostles answered, "We must obey God rather than men."

John 19:11 ESV "Jesus answered him, "You would have no authority over me at all unless it had been given you from above. Therefore he who delivered me over to you has the greater sin."

Racism/Sexual Identity-In the child development ecology textbook Child, Family, School, Community Socialization, and support 10ᵗʰ Edition by Roberta M. Berns, an article in the textbook states,

"That all men are created equal, that they are endowed by their CREATOR with certain unalienable rights, that among these are Life, Liberty and the pursuit of Happiness. This quote from the Declaration of Independence reflects the basic philosophy of a democratic society. Time has proven, however, that race and ethnicity are examples of diverse dimensions characterized by inequality. These determine how the United States distributes resources, such as school funding, grants to communities, scholarships, and more. The U.S Bureau of the Census has delineated the following racial classification requiring all federal agencies to use these categories on their data collection and analysis:

1. American Indian and Alaskan Native
2. Asian
3. Black or African American
4. Native Hawaiian and other Pacific Islander
5. White

Hispanics/Latinos are a separate classification because they are an ethnic group, rather than a single race, and distinguished by culture. Thus, each of the race classifications has a subcategory of Hispanic and non-Hispanic. The diverse dimensions of race and ethnicity are significant ways people define themselves and others. They impact relationships, neighborhoods, schools, work, politics, and the media." (Berns, P. 53)

Universities push affirmative action, 'life challenges,' and racial classifications in order to admit minorities-not because they're smarter than their white or Asian counterparts, but because they're minorities. They look for ways to admit underqualified students in place of qualified ones. Why not instead push for better achievement from minority students? Isn't it racist to imply that minorities cannot live up to the challenge? "University faculties love racial tension. They can't bear the idea that conservatives might be right about creating a color-blind society in place of a special treatment one." (Shapiro).

There is also such a thing as race-based testing in the public-school districts. If you are someone of color your proficiency level is lowered for people of color to make a proficiency level, so the school districts get more money. I then ask students is this unethical, racist, why would school districts not have everyone at the same level. Students discuss in small groups then we discuss whole class. The student's initial response is that this is wrong and the level of proficiency should be the same for all. This is when I inform my students that I had a 6th grader who had migrated from Mexico and had never been to school before. He is at a first-grade reading level. If his proficiency level is lowered and the school gets more money than they will have more resources to help this 6th grade student. Is it okay then that the proficiency level is lowered? This is when some students start to see the reality of school districts, testing, and federal money and how it can be a sticky situation.

All human beings in the world today are classified as Homo sapiens. Scientists today admit that, biologically, there really is only one race of humans. For instance, a scientist at the Advancement of Science Convention in Atlanta stated, "Race is a social construct derived mainly from perceptions conditioned by events of recorded history, and it has no basic biological reality." This person went on to say, "Curiously enough, the idea comes very close to being of American manufacture" (Hotz). The Bible does not even use the word race in reference to people, but it does describe all human beings as being of "one blood" (Acts 17:26). This of course emphasizes that we are all related, as all humans are descendants of the first man, Adam (1 Corinthians 15:45), who was created in the image of God (Genesis 1:26–27). The Last Adam, Jesus Christ (1 Corinthians 15:45) also became a descendant of Adam. Any descendant of Adam can be saved because our mutual relative by blood (Jesus) died and rose again. This is why the gospel can (and should) be preached to all tribes and nations. Slavery in the bible is not based on skin tone but on land ownership and marriage. For example, you were to work on a piece of land for 7 years before the land could be yours. You had to work on your future father in laws land for 7 years before you were married. Harsh slavery was shown as wrong in the bible when God asked Moses to lead his people out of Egypt and into the promise land. The Israelites were mistreated as slaves and God wanted his people to be free. In the story of the Tower of Babel God created different people groups with different languages, not races. The Tower of Babel story illustrates the true origins of racial diversity and combats divisive theories such as Critical race theory that is promoted in the education system and politicians in the Western nations. "While most evolutionists are probably not racists, the philosophy they hold is inherently racist, implying that some people groups are more closely related to apes than others" (Ken Ham). Whether or not you agree with Ken's assessment of evolution's racist roots, this is a good example of critical race theory in action. The individuals, Ken agrees, aren't racist, but they are taking part in a system that upholds racism. Critical Race Theory argues that society is divided into striations of power and in the United States, those striations have historically been divided along racial lines in ways that continue to affect our lives today. In other words, while a more traditional view of racism holds that individuals can be racist, critical race theory argues that systems can also be racist, whether or not the people who take part in them hold deliberately racist views. Critical race theory violates a biblical worldview by suggesting that people are essentially defined by their race or class rather than by their individual acts and attitudes. Please read (Jeremiah 31:31-34 and Revelations 20:11-13). Critical Race theory incorrectly emphasizes intersectional categories such as gender, race, sexual preference, and economic status above and beyond a person's own choices and responsibilities. "There is neither Jew nor Greek, neither slave nor free, nor male and female, for you are all one in Christ Jesus (Galatians 3:28 NIV)." Critical Race Theory also conflicts with a biblical approach to objective, absolute truth. This includes suggesting that an oppressed person's feelings matter more than what the oppressor has actual done or intended (1 Corinthians 4:4; 10:29). Critical Race Theory replaces an individual and personal relationship with God with a collectivistic system. When and Where prejudices are found in the church, they should be addressed according to sound doctrine, not according to an inherently unbiblical approach such as Critical Race Theory. Our schools, government, politicians want to indoctrinate our children with Critical Race Theory.

The facts are clear:

1. We came from one man.
"The first man (was) Adam" (1 Cor. 15:45). We know from God's Word that all people descended from one man, Adam. The Y-Chromosome contains DNA that is passed directly from father to son. We would predict that Y-chromosome DNA would be similar in all men alive today. Scientific research on Y-Chromosome DNA seems to show this.

2. We came from one woman.
"Eve...was the mother of all living" (Gen. 3:20). We know from God's Word that all people descended from one woman, Eve. Mitochondrial DNA is passed directly from mother to child. We would predict that mitochondrial DNA would be similar in all people alive today. Scientific research on mitochondrial DNA seems to bear this out.

3. We are fully human from fertilization.
All the genetic information to make an individual is present at fertilization, so right from the start, a fertilized human egg cell is totally human. There is no biological basis for drawing any other line for when we become human. Every human is fully human, from fertilization to the end of life.

4. There is only one race of humans.
All of us descended from the first two people-with a common ancestry, we are not different biological races. However, the Bible makes it clear there are two spiritual races (those who trust Christ and those who don't). Charles Darwin's ideas on evolution originally divided people into races. It's important to understand that every human has the same basic skin color. Any differences in that color are simply a matter of the shade of our skin-how light or dark we are. Imagine you are going to the store with someone to buy paint to paint your fence. Let's say you want to paint your fence brown. You can pick a light brown, a darker brown, or a really dark brown. It's

sort of like that with people. There are no truly "black" or "white" people. All humans are actually shades of brown because of the pigment in our skin. This pigment is what changes the shade of this one main color. The name of this pigment is melanin because of the problems in their genes. Attached is a video link on Grace Relations with Charles Ware that I found enlightening and phenomenal when it comes to race and Christianity. I have been told by my superiors that even suggesting this link as an option to view on student's own time is HATE speech because the evolutionist in my classroom would view it that way. There is a big difference between first amendment right of free speech and violence. You either believe in free speech or you don't. Free speech is essential to our democracy and promotes self-government. Hate speech is not a legal term. Censorship does more harm than good.

https://youtu.be/mITCu7eRlxE

Side note- If you want to read more on the issue of slavery in the Bible, I strongly suggest you read The New Answers Book 3 by Ken Ham. It gives a brief history of slavery, slavery in the Bible, harsh slavery, Christians leading the Fight to abolish slavery, and race. The gist of it was that slavery in the bible was not based on skin color, but based on working off a debt or wanting to marry one's daughter. Harsh slavery was never supported as shown in the Egyptian/Israelite story where God sent Moses to let his people go. Some much historical and biblical detail all of which is extremely important. Trust me get the book.

In the book <u>One Race One Blood</u> by Ken Hamm and Charles Ware it states the following:

> 'Rev. Jesse Jackson says the birth of gays and lesbians for same sex marriage is not to be compared to the fight of African Americans civil rights.' (Hutcherson, The Seattle times. March 29, 2004). African Americans' struggle for civil rights in the United States is rooted

in systemic fact that there were human beings created in the image of God who were being denied rights guaranteed to them in the U.S. Constitution. On the other hand, same-sex relationships, whether multiple or monogamous, are biblically and morally wrong. Such relationships are contrary to the devein design, non-reproductive, declared to be wrong, changeable, and never positively regulated in the Bible. To equate the created essence of a person with behavioral moral choices is flawed thinking. The attempt of homosexual activists to form a holy union between the African American civil rights struggle and the homosexual agenda is a marriage made on earth, not in heaven. The Bible clearly argues for one human race. With equal clarity it identifies homosexuality as morally wrong. "Morality" is not some philosophical, abstract concept. Things that are morally wrong have serious repercussions in practical life. Biblical morality is rooted in the fact that life was designed to be lived with certain paraments if we step outside of those paraments the consequences are never positive. Homosexuality hurts. Beyond the biblical and psychological aspects, it hurts society from a public health and economic perspective. 'In the United States, men who have sex with men constituted 70 percent of all estimated HIV-infections cases among male adult and adolescents in 2004, even though only about 5 to 7 percent of male adults' adolescents in the United States identify themselves as men who have sex with men' (CDC July 2006). 'Of the 756,399 American men who acquired full-blown AIDS from the beginning of the epidemic in this country through 2004, 506,213 (66.92 percent) were in the risk category of men who have sex with men.' (CDC, 2005).

Here are some thought-provoking questions, does our culture change science? You are either XX a girl or XY a boy. Do we change science to fit the culture and social factors? Is gender dysphoria in a large population? How many people with gender dysphoria also have mental illness? Is changing your gender a mental illness? With LGBTQAI+ community with a high number of suicides can having a relationship with God help them? How many people that have decided to change their gender regret it? Is the Black Lives Matter Movement an organization that God sees as oppressed and stand for biblical truth? What is the development of a child who grows up in a racist home? What is the development of the child who grows up with a guardian who is a part of the LGBTQAI+ community? Since these are sin issues, they will not be brought up in a home based on Biblical truth. They will struggle with moral and ethical decisions. What does the Bible say about homosexual behavior and gay marriage? Study the following verses: Genesis 2:18-25; Leviticus 18:22, Mark 10:6; Romans 1:26-27; 1 Corinthians 6:9-10; Timothy 1:9-10. "Bible's authority has been increasingly undermined, as much of the Church has compromised with the idea of millions of years (this began before Darwin) and has thus begun reinterpreting Genesis...The Bible has lost respect in people's eyes (both within and without the Church) to the extent that the culture as a whole now does not take the Bible's morality seriously at all. The increasing acceptance of homosexual behavior and gay marriage is a symptom of the loss of biblical authority, and is primarily due to the compromise the Church has made with the secular world's teaching on origins." (Ken Ham-The New Answers Book 2). The battle against gay marriage will ultimately be lost just like the battle against abortion unless the church and the culture return to the absolute authority beginning in Genesis. Then and only then will there be a true foundation for the correct doctrine of marriage-one man for one woman for life.

Gender ideology does harm children because it teaches them something that goes completely against God's good design. Beginning in Genesis, we know that God created "male and female" (Genesis 1:27) and that design was "very good" (Genesis 1:31).

Now in our sin-cursed and fallen world (Genesis 3), some people struggle with their maleness or femaleness, and these people need compassion and love. But this does not mean that we should reject God's design and simply do what feels right. Emotions—however strong—do not replace the absolute truth of God's Word. It is God's Word that must serve as the starting point for our thinking as we lovingly come alongside others and share the gospel of Jesus Christ with them. We need to be proactive in teaching our children to start their thinking with God's Word. The secular world is growing increasingly aggressive in promoting an ethic where everyone does what's right in their own eyes. (Judges 21:25); many young people, even those in the church, are being drawn into this kind of thinking. We need to point our children continually to God's Word as the firm foundation for determining morality. We can't simply do what's right in our own eyes—we are accountable to our Creator! If people only knew the Joy and Peace you have when you have a relationship with God. "Do not be conformed to this world, but be transformed by the renewal of your mind, that by testing you may discern what is the will of God, what is good and acceptable and perfect" (Romans 12:2 ESV). And we also often need to be reminded of the good news of the gospel. Transgender individuals—like all of us—need to hear this good news. They need to know that "all have sinned and fall short of the glory of God" (Romans 3:23 NIV), but that "He made Him who knew no sin to be sin for us, that we might become the righteousness of God in Him" (2 Corinthians 5:21 ESV) in order that "if you confess with your mouth the Lord Jesus and believe in your heart that God has raised Him from the dead, you will be saved" (Romans 10:9 ESV).

Side Note- In regards to pride month, pride is perhaps the most slippery of temptations to cope with. You may not have a problem with pride, and be proud that you don't have a problem with pride and in that process, you have just developed a pride problem. Pride is a sin. True happiness comes from serving Christ, not your own selfish desires. Here are just a few quotes in Child Development textbook The Developing Person through Childhood and Adolescence 12th edition in regards to LGBTQ.

On page 436 it states, "However LGBTQ youth have a higher risk of depression and anxiety, for reasons from every level of Bronfenbrenner's ecological system approach."

On page 437 it states, "Every study Finds that parental communication influences adolescent behavior. Effective programs of sex education explicitly require parental participation." "Religious values also have some influence, but again the impact comes from general messages about respect and love rather than from specifics."

Page 444" Suicide rates are seven times higher for LGBTQ youth than others."

Page 271" Sex and gender issues are particularly salient When a child is transgender, Identity as being a gender other than the one assigned at birth."

Page 272" Unlike in that family, some parents, during early childhood except their child's Insistence That they are transgender. A study of 36 Transgendered children, whose parents accepted their transition to the other sex before age six, compared with them their siblings and with cisgender Children who were the same age."

Nature Vs. Nurture Describes how much a person's characteristics are formed by either "nature" or "nurture." Nature means innate biological factors (namely genetics). While nurture can refer to upbringing or life experiences. In regards to sexual orientation or gender what roles could nature vs. nurture have. Are you born with it, genetically prone to get it, or is it more from your upbringing and life experiences? I have been told by my superiors that I am not allowed to use this example of nature vs nurture as it could be offensive to others.

Eric Erickson created 8 stages of psychosocial development. In order to find one's identity, one must have a positive outcome in the previous stages. The first stage is Trust Vs. Mistrust (Does one generally trust people or distrust them?); the second stage autonomy versus shame and doubt (Am I confident I can be independent, or am I doubtful about my ability to be independent?); the third stage Initiative versus guilt (Do I feel good about starting new things or meeting new people, or do I feel guilty?); the fourth stage industry versus inferiority (Do I feel competent about my abilities, or inferior?). The fifth stage is the identity vs. Role confusion (Who am I and what is my role in life?) It is during this stage that one is trying out roles and using the reactions of others to judge how well the roles fit their self-concept. "Preadolescent children who are on the brink of entering the identity-versus-role confusion stage look to the peer's group for their identity. The group's symbols and rituals (ways of dressing, ways of behaving, attitudes, opinions), as well as its approval and support, help define what is good and what is bad, thereby contributing to the development of ego identity. Identifying with a group and excluding those who are not like the members of the group helps children identify who they are by affirming who they are not. Young people in this 5th stage begin to derive an identity from their experiences, their abilities, and their goals. They begin to look within themselves rather than to others for who they are. The peer group, then, serves to mediate between the individual and society, playing a powerful role in shaping the individual's identity." (Adler & Adler, 1998).

My question to college students is this-Why are very young children having genital mutilation to change their gender when they are not yet at the Identity stage yet?

Deuteronomy 22:5 ESV "A woman shall not wear a man's garment, nor shall a man put on a woman's cloak, for whoever does these things is an abomination to the Lord your God.

Genesis 1:27 ESV "So God created man in his own image, in the image of God he created him; male and female he created them."

Romans 1:24-27 ESV "Therefore, God gave them up in the lusts of their hearts to impurity, to the dishonoring of their bodies among themselves, because they exchanged the truth about God for a lie and worshiped and served the creature rather than the Creator, who is blessed forever! Amen. For this reason, God gave them up to dishonorable passions. For their women exchanged natural relations for those that are contrary to nature; and the men likewise gave up natural relations with women and were consumed with passion for one another, men committing shameless acts with men and receiving in themselves the due penalty for their error."

The following story is from the Child Development college textbook <u>Child, Family, and Community Family-Centered Early Care and Education</u> by Janet Gonzalez-Mena 7th Edition Chapter 12 Page 273.

> Michael's Family. The fourth family has one child enrolled in the child care center. Three-year-old Michael is a quiet boy with long dark eyelashes that sweep down on his cheeks when he lowers his eyes, which he does a good deal of the time. He is cautious and slow to warm up to people, but his slightly withdrawn manner has captured the hearts of the staff.
>
> Michael's parents, Margaret and Beth, are a lesbian couple. Although the child comes every day, the staff has barely talked to his parents. They seem to move in and out of the center like shadows. Margaret usually brings Michael. She is friendly to staff but always in a hurry. Because some of the staff members have mixed feelings about this couple, several are rather glad the women are so unobtrusive and seemingly unwilling to engage in conversation. However, one staff member has strong feelings about the bias this family may be experiencing in the center. She wants to change the atmosphere and be sure that the parents and the child feel comfortable and accepted. She has begun to introduce the subject of anti-bias regularly at staff meetings, and this has brought forth some discomfort among the staff. At the last meeting she pointed out that although the program is committed to "celebrating diversity," there is no physical evidence in the center that lesbian and gay couples are considered normal families. Pictures abound (on the walls and in books) that show all kinds of family configurations, except same-sex

parents. No books in the center show gay or lesbian families.

"What can we do to make school more comfortable for and accepting of Michael and his family?" was the teacher's question to the rest of the staff.

"Good question," responded one teacher. "This is something we should talk about. I'm concerned about Michael," she added emphatically.

"I'm concerned about his parents as well!" said the first teacher, equally emphatically. "What can we do to raise the comfort level?"

The staff is still working on this question because they are in conflict with each other what should be done. They can't even agree about the idea of bringing books and pictures of families like Michael's. Some feel strongly that it's an equity issue they are discussing; others are taking a moral or religious stance. In the meantime, it's easy to see the discomfort level rise in Michael and his parents as they pick up unspoken messages from various staff members.

Although Michael's parents have many traits of the successful family, they are unable to benefit from what the staff might have to offer them to increase their knowledge of child development and family relations because of limited communication.

Here are some questions addressed to college students in regards to this story:

Should Christian teachers be forced to teach something against their beliefs? Should Christians be uncomfortable to make others comfortable? How can Christians show love to a family as God calls us to Love our neighbor as ourselves, but not compromise our beliefs? How did God/Jesus show love to those who were unbelievers or sinful?

I worked as an ABA Specialist (Applied Behavior Analysis) for three years. I would go into the homes of autistic families ranging from the ages of 2-6. As a therapist we are looking to improve communication with these kids and their families as well as a variation of skills. My first day on the job I was working with a family who was low income, inter racial, lesbian couple whose parenting style was Permissive-No discipline in the home, gave the children whatever they wanted. The child I was there to see was strapped to a chair at the table, he was about 2. He had an older sibling who would bang his head on glass until his head began to bleed. The older child was about 6 and was outside with the blind diabetic aunt and was beating her with a stick till the point the aunt was bleeding. The aunt came wobbling in and I shut the door blocking the child from entering the home. The door was half glass at the top so you could see through the door. The child began to throw objects at the door. The child I was there to see had unstrapped himself and began to bite my hind leg as I was blocking the door. One of the mommies was on bedrest and very pregnant and the other mommy was at work. I knew nothing about this family and had not even built up a rapport with the kids and family. There should have been a case manager there. I left that home early and cried in my car and called my husband because I wanted to quit. Maybe the job gave me the worst case to see if I would stay. Have you ever been in a position that you wanted to quit a job, but you couldn't because bills were piling up. We were in a financial mess and I had no other choice but to work. I ended up staying with that family for 3 years. I ended up following in love with a family very different than my own. I led by example showing them another way on parenting. Even though are life styles being completely different I wanted to show love to my neighbor. The child and that family had improved so much and I was thankful to be a part of it.

"One of the teachers of the law came and heard them debating. Noticing that Jesus had given them a good answer, he asked him,

'Of all the commandments, which is the most important?' 'The most important one,' answered Jesus, 'is this: 'Hear, O Israel: The Lord our God, the lord is one. Love the Lord your God with all your heart and with all your soul and with all your mind and with all your strength.' The second is this: 'Love your neighbor as yourself. 'There is no commandment greater than these."-Mark 12:28-31 NLT. True love is willing to get involved. Is someone close to you toying with a sin that could ruin his or her life? Be sure your own life is an open book before God; then confront that individual in love. True love is willing to confront, to discipline, and to get personally involved. In Nehemiah 13:25 he had to get personally involved. As Christians we are to teach, correct, rebuke.

INTERETHNIC (RACIAL) AND INTERFAITH (RELIGIOUS) FAMILIES

All of this information came from a Child Development College Textbook <u>Child, Family, School, and Community Socialization</u> and support 10th edition by Robert M. Berns. In the textbook it states:

>"When people with different heritages marry and have families, they face certain challenges not experienced by those couples who have similar backgrounds. This is also true of parents who adopt children of a different color or ethnicity than theirs. Because interethnic families differ in physical traits, such as color or ethnic features, they are more likely than interfaith families to face the prejudices of others. In addition to the challenges of dealing with stereotyping, both interethnic and interfaith parents must deal with their cultural contrasts, reflected by different values, communications style, perception of appropriate gender roles, beliefs about parenting, and so on. They must decide how to carry on their cultural or religious traditions with their children. They must also enable their children to form a sense of identity" (Crohn, 1995). "The number of interethnic and interfaith families has increased" (Hitlin, Brown, & Elder, 2006). "Mixed marriages (interethnic or interfaith) are more complicated relationships than

are those between people of similar backgrounds (Crohn, 1995). People with different religious backgrounds may be attracted to one another because their difference are interesting. However, the novelty and excitement of cultural contrasts can turn into an embitterment of cultural clashes, especially when families (of orientation and procreation) are brought into the picture" (Crohn, 1995).

"September is the Jewish High Holiday season, which is a ten-day period from Rosh Hashana, the Jewish New Year, to Yom Kippur, the Day of Atonement. During this time, Jews are supposed to review their moral behavior and ask those people who were wronged, as well as God, for forgiveness. This time of the year is so significant, that even non practicing Jews attend synagogue services. Every High Holiday season since Michelle a Jew, married Robert, a Catholic, she felt sad and nostalgic. The couple did not belong to a synagogue or a church and Michelle missed the sense of community and traditional celebrations she experienced growing up. For example, her favorite holiday was Passover, a time when Jewish people remember their historical roots telling the story of the flight from Egypt across the desert to Jerusalem. The whole family gathers around the table and eats special food to commemorate events in the story.

When Michelle married Robert, religion was not much of an issue. They loved each other and so they thought they would work things out as they went along. They were married by a justice of the people in the beautiful garden of a local hotel. They felt that since they paid for the wedding, their parents couldn't pressure them to do a religious ceremony.

Although Robert was baptized as a Catholic (reborn) when he was an infant, he was not devout. He did partake of Holy Communion as a child, believing he was receiving Jesus's blood, body, soul, and divinity, and as a teen he was confirmed (accepting responsibility of following the tenets of the Church). When he went away to college, he stopped going to confession. He did maintain his belief in Jesus as the son of God and that the Bible was God's word. As a child, he loved celebrating Christmas, Jesus's birthday, but really felt part of the Christian community on Easter, the day of Jesus's resurrection.

While Michelle's and Robert's parents warned the couple about the problems of an interfaith marriage, such as lack of religious indemnity and how their faiths would be passed to their children, the parents only became intrusive on holidays. When Michelle became pregnant, the real pressure began (not only form parents and relatives, but from friends, too). The couple was stressed-they started arguing about values, beliefs, whose childhood was more meaningful, and so on. They decided to go to a marriage counselor who specialized in working with interfaith couples. They each wanted to retain the important traditions of their respective religions. The counselor advised them this might be confusing to a child and suggested that they join an interfaith couple's support group to learn what worked and did not work for other families (Berns, P. 136).

Some questions I would ask the college students and that are directly from the textbook would be:

What influences did your religious heritage have on your beliefs and values?

What traditions from your religious heritage have you incorporated into your adult life?

Erikson's-Identity Versus Role confusion (Who am I, and what is my role in life?)

What is the impact on marriage and family when parents have had different upbringing regarding customs, values, beliefs, and traditions?

CHILD DEVELOPMENT IN EDUCATION-SHOULD RELIGION BE IN SCHOOLS?

Warning-There is so much to talk about from an educational perspective and a biblical one. Short answer- Religion in schools is already being taught-let me explain, very long explanation.

In the college textbook, <u>The Developing Person Through Childhood and Adolescence twelfth Edition</u> by Kathleen Stassen Berger it poses the question on page 331 "Should public education be free of religion to avoid bias toward one religion or another? In the United States, thousands of parochial schools were founded when Catholics perceived Protestant bias in public schools. In the past 20 years, many Catholic schools have closed, but schools teaching other religions—-Judaism, Islam, evangelical Christianity—-have opened." "Religious education also varies. The U.S Constitution forbids overt teaching of religion in public schools (although, of course, children can pray, express beliefs, or wear religious symbols), but other nations believe religious education is part of learning. In the Unites States, many private schools teach religion, and parents sometimes choose them for precisely that reason." (Berger P. 323) This is when I pose the question to college students, is separation of church and state in the constitution and what does Thomas Jefferson letter really say?

Let's start with the term Religion. Religion does not necessarily mean a God. Atheism is a Religion that does not believe in a God. Evolution is a form of Religion that gives birth to Atheism. If you believe in the millions of years scum of the earth to animals to eventually man than you don't believe that God created the world in 6 days including animals and Adam and Eve. If you believe in the billion-year concept that earth was created by the Big Bang then you don't believe that God created night, day, stars, planets, land, and water. My point is this, you are already indoctrinated in the public school that teaches these theories that is a Religion. Atheism and Evolution is a religion without a God. But I'm sure you're scratching your head at this point and saying well Evolution and Big Bang are just theories and science and that is exactly my point. Science is Historical, Observable, and Experimental. How do we know that George Washington was the first president or that Jesus was born from a virgin, performed miracles, and was crucified. We only know these things because of the people that were there during that time that created factual records. This is historical science when we see historical records. Observation science is when you see something take place and document what you see and Experimental science is when you experiment and document your findings. Big Bang Theory and Evolution are not Historical-no one was around to write down factual findings, they were not observed. The only Experimental Science we have is fossil dating from dinosaur bones. Did you know that Creationists and evolutionist have the same facts? The facts are not what people argue or debate over. It's the interpretation of the facts that people argue about. One's interpretation depends on one's worldview. One's worldview depends on the presuppositions we have. Ultimately, there are only two foundations for our worldviews: God's word or man's word. A creation scientist and a secular scientist can agree on how deep the Grand Canyon is. They agree the Colorado river flows through the canon and any such river does cause some erosion of rocks. This is observational science. However, when secularists claim the Colorado River eroded the Canyon over millions of years, that is now in the realm of historical science. No one was there to see what actually happened. Secularists are not teaching student in our public education system to think correctly about science and the past. Sadly, generations of students are being brainwashed by secularists who are committed to their religion of evolution and don't want students to think critically about the origins issue. I always use the pandemic examples. There is science that shows that the vaccines work, but there is also science that shows that they don't. There is science that shows that masks work, but there is also science that shows that they don't. You're looking at the scientists, not the science. If you're a scientist that believes in evolution then you're going to interpret data to fit your cognitive theory. If you're a scientist that believes in creation, you're going to do the same. What if I told you there was more science that proves creation would you believe me, probably not since you may be an evolutionist.

From a Christian timeline there is 2,000 years between us and Jesus, 2,000 years between Jesus and Abraham, and 2,000 years between Abraham and Adam and Eve. Which means that the earth is only a little over 6,000 years old. There is a whole book on genealogy in the Bible, not the most exciting to read, but important to see. Dinosaurs were created during the same day that Adam and Eve were. The term dinosaur meaning giant lizard was a term man created much later. In the Bible in the book of Job describes Behemoth which in the description is what a dinosaur would look like. The passage Job 40:15-24 certainly suggests a large animal, and no known living animal fits the passage adequately. The tail of Behemoth is compared to a cedar for its great size, and there is nothing in the context which contradicts this possibility, some type of extinct dinosaur should still be considered a perfectly reasonable possibility. We lived in a perfect world until Adam and Eve sinned. Dinosaurs did not eat meat they only ate plants and so did Adam and Eve. There was no death, disease, or destruction until AFTER Adam and Eve sinned. Dinosaurs could not have lived millions of years ago because death had not occurred yet. The mass extinction of dinosaurs actually happened during Noah's flood. The account for Noah's flood is in Genesis 7-8 this is an actual event in earths history. We find the geological evidence is absolutely in harmony with the Word of God. As the ocean waters flooded over the continents, they must have buried plants and animals in rapid succession. These rapidly deposited sediment layers were spread across vast areas, preserving fossils of sea creatures in layers that are high above current sea level. The sand and other sediments in these layers were transported long distances from their original sources. We know that many of these sedimentary strata were laid down in rapid succession because we don't find evidence of slow erosion between the strata. Jesus Christ our Creator (John 1:1-3; Colossians 1:16-17), who is the Truth and would never tell us a lie, said that during the "days of Noah" (Mathew 24;37; Luke 17:26-27) "Noah entered the ark" and "the Flood came and took them all away" (Matthew 24: 38-39 NIV). He spoke of these events as real, literal history, describing a global Flood that destroyed all land life not on the ark. Therefore, we must believe what He told us, rather than believe the ideas of fallible scientist who weren't there to see what happened in the earth's past. We shouldn't be surprised then the geological evidence in God's world agrees exactly with Gods Word, affirmed by Jesus Christ. Evolutionary timeline will tell you the ice age occurred 2.4 million years ago, but it was only about 4,000 years ago after Noah's flood. Noah's flood is what caused the ice age. Scientists use a technique called radiometric dating to estimate the ages of rocks, fossils, and the earth. Many people have been led to believe that radiometric dating methods have proved the earth to be billions of years old. This has caused many in the church to reevaluate the biblical creation account, specifically the meaning of the word "day" in Genesis 1. Contrary to popular misconception, carbon dating is not used to date rocks at millions of years old. You will find that carbon dating supports a young earth. All radiometric dating methods are based on assumptions about events that happened in the past. If the assumptions are accepted as true (as is typically done in the evolutionary dating processes), results can be biased toward a desired age. In the reported ages given in textbooks and other journals, these evolutionary assumptions have not been questioned, while results inconsistent with long ages have been censored. When the assumptions were evaluated and shown faulty, the results supported the biblical account of a global flood and young earth. Christians should not be afraid of radiometric dating methods. Carbon-14 dating is really the friend of Christians, and it supports a young earth.

Can you be a real scientist and be a Christian? The answer is yes.

> "Isaac Newton (1642-1727)-He had a profound knowledge of, and faith in, the Bible. Carl Linnaeus (1707-1778) and Nicolaus Steno (1631-1686)-Believed the Genesis creation account. Today there are many PhD scientist who reject evolution and believe that God created in 6 days, a few thousand years ago. Russ Humphreys, Johan Baumgardner, Dr. Raymond Damadian just to name a few. Creationist can indeed be real scientist." (Ken Ham-The New Anwers Book 2).

In 6th grade you go over the ancient civilizations. Ancient China you discuss Buddhism, Hinduism, and Confucius. In Ancient Egypt you discuss mummification and the afterlife. Ancient Greece and all their Gods are discussed in 6th Grade and again in 9th grade. The stone age period and the hominids are discussed in 6th grade as well. In the 6th grade curriculum is also the ancient Roman civilization, but it is skipped over. Can you tell me why? If you're a Bible reader you know why. Jesus is discussed. I taught 6th grade for one school year, when asked why we skip over they stated it was because it was not in the common core state standards and a teacher stated that we would most likely need written permission from parents to teach that. This is where I scratched my head. We would need written permission for Ancient Rome but not on Hominids. This particular school site was really heavy into visuals and wanted drawing of the monkey to man theory on my wall. I am so glad I got out of public-school teaching. Way too much indoctrination for me.

As you can see Religion is very much taught in our schools in a hidden way through evolution, big bang (which gives birth to Atheist) and other anti-biblical indoctrinations such as CRT, LGBTQAI+. There are too many denominations to count but here are just a few off the top of my head, Catholics, Protestant, Evangelical, Baptist, Pentecostal, Mennonite, Lutheran, Jehovah

Witness, Mormons, Scientology, all these denominations have different practices and some of them are not biblical and a few I would consider cults. "Religion Pluralism flourishes in the United States. There are about 2,000 religious' groups, and with the influx of immigrants from Asia, Africa, and the Middle East, non-Western religions such as Islam, Hinduism, and Buddhism are joining the ranks of Protestantism, Catholicism, and Judaism" (Gollnick & Chinn, 2012). It would be time consuming and unnecessary to teach about the various denominations. I do not think that Bible teaching should be done in school as teachers may cherry pick and we will have many false teachers. But I also think we should not have evolution, big bang, LGBTQAI+ or CRT. There are certain aspects of the Bible such as the Fruits of the Spirit that can be a universal concept in public school. "But the fruit of the Spirit is love, joy, peace, patience, kindness, goodness, faithfulness, gentleness, and self-control. Against such things there is no law. Those who belong to Christ Jesus have crucified the sinful nature with its passions and desires. Since we live by the Spirit, let us keep in step with the Spirit. Let us not become conceited, provoking, and envying each other" (Galatians 5: 22-26 New International Version). I would think there would be a lot less suicides amongst kids if we showed love, Peace, and kindness. There would be fewer school shootings if we practice self-control and joy. We would have better teachers if we practiced gentleness and patience.

In chapter 6 of the Child Development Ecology textbook <u>Child, Family, School, Community Socialization, and support 10th Edition</u> by Roberta M. Berns, it states that,

> "The first amendment to the Constitution guarantees freedom of religion and requires separation of church and state. This means educational policy mandates that public schools cannot promote a particular religion, nor can they inhibit religious beliefs. The word 'God' is in many government documents, such as the Declaration of Independence and money. In 1956, Congress adopted 'In God we trust' as

the official motto of the Unites States. This policy has been debated throughout the country's history, as exemplified by such issues as school prayer, appropriate science curriculum, extracurricular activities in public school facilities, and school vouchers." "Although political ideology in the United States advocates separation of church and state (including public school), the two often intersect. For example, the phrase 'One nation, under God' is now in the pledge of Allegiance, and the phrase 'In God we trust' appears on the U.S currency. The degree to which religious ideologies intersect with public school curricula and policies is significant in the socialization of all children who attend public school. Issues that have been controversial are school prayer, the curriculum (teaching evolution, sex education), censorship of certain books, and the celebration of certain holidays. Teachers need to be sensitive to the values of the families in the community in the context of a diverse society, while at the same time implementing the educational goals of the school district. Sometimes the line between secular and nonsecular education is a fine one and must be determined by the courts. Legally, public school may teach the Bible as part of the history of literature (as a story), but they may not teach it as Religion (as a holy document). Reading of scriptures and reciting prayers is a violation. Public schools may teach the scientific theory of evolution, but not biblical creationism. Dismissing children an hour early from public school for religious instruction is permitted. How are secular and nonsecular distinguished? Secular deal with worldly experiences, nonsecular with spiritual ones. How can the Bible represent both, yet only be allowed to be taught as literature? Literature consists of writings in prose or verse, whereas the Bible also consist of sacred religious scriptures. Therefore, biblical stories can be taught minus their spiritual messages." (Berns P. 214)

President George W. Bush established the Center for Faith-Based and Community Initiative to provide opportunities for faith based and community organizations to apply to the U.S. Department of Education for grants, such as programs for early reading, family literacy, and after school activities, in order to help ensure that no child is left behind.

This is where in my child development classroom I would encourage students to look at Thomas Jefferson's letter closely to understand the meaning of separation of church and state. Separation of Church and State is **not** a part of the original U.S. Constitution of 1787, as most people falsely believe, or in any of its amendments. The idea of a "wall of separation" between church and state came from a private letter from President Thomas Jefferson, and it has sadly been misused to slowly, but surely, eliminate Christianity from the public sector-and replace it with an anti-God religion. The Establishment Clause in the First Amendment was intended to **protect** the church from the (federal) government, **not** the government from the church. Therefore, no "national" church or religion is allowed to be established by the federal government. The first Amendment states, "Congress shall make no law respecting an establishment of religion or prohibiting the free exercise thereof." You can see that the "separation of church and state" phrase is nowhere in the Amendment (or the rest of the Constitution). The 1802 letter from Jefferson was sent to the Danbury Baptist Association in Connecticut in response to the groups letter to him. Jefferson was trying to assure the Baptists that the federal government would never be permitted to interfere with the church. In fact, in his letter, Jefferson states: "Believing with you that religion is a matter which lie solely between man and his God, that he owes account to none other for his faith or his worship, that the legitimate powers of government reach actions only, and not opinions, I contemplate with sovereign reverence that act of the whole American people which declared that their legislature should make no law respecting an establishment of religion or prohibiting the free exercise thereof, thus building a wall of separation between church and state." "Separation of church and state" is now used to protect the government from the influence of the church—establishing a policy of freedom "from" religion, which has become "separation of Christianity and state." This would have been an entirely foreign and unintended concept to the Founding Fathers. Sadly, most Americans (Christians included) have also been duped into believing that the so-called "separation of church and state" requires eliminating the Christian God and creating a neutral situation. But there is no such position as neutrality. Indeed, one is either for Christ or against Him (Matthew 12:30)! The religion of naturalism (atheism) has been imposed on the public education system, and on the culture. For instance, science textbooks in the public schools now typically define science as naturalism (atheism): "Science requires repeatable observations and testable hypotheses. These standards restrict science to a search for natural causes for natural phenomena . . .. Supernatural explanations of natural events are simply outside the bounds of science" (Campell, Williamson, Heyden, P.38). In keeping with this pronouncement, these books teach molecules-to-man evolution, based only on unproven natural processes, as fact! In other words, they have eliminated the supernatural and replaced it with naturalism. They have eliminated the Christian worldview and replaced it with a secular, atheistic one! Sadly, because many Christians have falsely believed that there can be a neutral position, and have also been duped regarding the so-called "separation of church and state," they are not prepared to stand on the Word of God boldly and unashamedly as they confront issues like abortion, "gay" marriage, racism, etc. By shrinking back, believers have allowed the secularists to impose their **anti-God atheistic religion on the public schools**—and the culture. "When the public school system threw out prayer, bible reading, creation, and the Ten commandments, they didn't throw out religion. They replaced the Christian worldview influence with an atheistic one. The public schools, by and large, now teach that everything a student learns about science, history, etc., has nothing to do with God-it can all be explained without any supernatural reference. THIS IS A RELIGIOUS VIEW-an anti-Christian view with which students are being indoctrinated. Humanists know that naturalistic evolution is foundational to their religion-their worldview that everything can be explained without God. That is why they are so emotional when it comes to the topic of creation/evolution." (Ken Ham The New Answers Book 3). Based on the U.S Constitution, no single religion should be endorsed in a government-run school. If no one stands up to challenge these ideas, the schools will continue to indoctrinate students with their religious beliefs of humanists. If teaching creation was mandated it would most likely be taught poorly by a teacher who does not understand it. Teachers should be allowed the **ACADEMIC FREEDOM** to present various models of the history of life on earth and teach the strengths and weaknesses of those models. Politics only allows for evolution. "Dr Michael Ruse, from the Department of Philosophy at the University of Guelph in Ontario, is a philosopher of science, particularly of the evolutionary sciences. He is the author of several books on Darwinism and evolutionary theory and in an article in the National Post he wrote:

> Evolution is promoted by its practitioners more than mere science. Evolution is promulgated as an ideology, a secular religion-a full fledged alterative to Christianity, with meaning and morality.

> ...Evolution is a religion. This was true of evolution in the beginning, and it is true of evolution still today. (Ken Ham-The New Answers Book 2).

HOMESCHOOLING AND CHILD DEVELOPMENT IN REGARDS TO FAITH

In the textbook <u>The Developing Person Through Childhood and Adolescence 12th Edition</u> by Kathleen Stasssen-Berger homeschooling is discussed on page 330. Question #4 states "Parents can choose to home-school their children, never sending them to school. In the United States, home-schooled children must learn certain subjects (reading, math, and so on), but each family decides schedules and discipline. About 2 percent of all U.S children were home-schooled in 2003 and about 3 percent in 2007. Since then, numbers have leveled off at between 3 and 4 percent (Grady, 2017; Ray, 2013; Snyder & Dillow, 2013). Home schooling requires intense family labor, typically provided by an educated, dedicated, patient mother in a two-parent family. The major disadvantage for home-schooled children is not academic (some have high test scores) but social: no classmates. To compensate, many parents plan activities with other home-schooling families. As I am writing this it is the year 2024 and I am positive that homeschool has increased drastically since the COVID scare. According to an article by Ken Ham "According to a poll in May 2020 a startling 40% of American families said they were more likely to homeschool their children after the lockdowns end. Well, that was back in May. In August of that same year a new poll has found that 82% of parents are at least considering keeping their children home through 2021" (Ken Ham August 12, 2020). Although there are times when my children need to understand when it is socially acceptable to discuss certain subjects my boys seem to have very little social problems.

Their friends complain that at times they are too talkative and annoying. They are outgoing social butterflies. If you keep your kids active in sports, youth groups, or kid activities, and plan play dates your kids will not grow up to be socially awkward because they were homeschooled. I would much rather have my kids be a little awkward than to be taught some of the antibiblical ideology the public schools teach. In our child development textbook it states, "School-age children can think and act morally, but they do not always do so because the hidden curriculum, or adult values, or peer pressure may lead them astray from their morals" (Berger P. 362). What hidden curriculum would cause students to astray from their morals? Is Evolutionary Theory, Big Bang Theory, Darwin's Theory, Critical Race Theory, LGBTQAI+ a moral education? What is a moral education and what would that look like? Where do Morals come from? These are questions I ask my college students as we discuss Kohlberg's Moral Development. Theres more on this topic later in this book.

It is a parent's fundamental right to make choices for their children when it comes to their education. Homeschooling is an alternative to a godless and immoral curriculum in public schools. Home school families should be protected from government regulations. Christian home school advocates are taking an active role in policies becoming laws. Home-schoolers are fighting for freedom and want to be left alone from government. Government should not dictate what is taught at home. Christian parents want to oversee the development and upbring of their children as they see fit. In Ohio, a child was removed from a home and placed with grandparents where Christian parents did not affirm the child's gender transition. Harvard Law professor Elizabeth Bartholet caused a national uproar for suggesting there ought to be a ban on homeschooling. Children belong to God and to the parents he ordained to take cere of these precious children. God graciously bestows children to husband and wife as an embodied expression of their covenantal union. The God who gives children to parents bestows on parents the earthly responsibility to care for them.

God ordained the family before he ordained the church. This

means that the family unit must be Christ centered and teaching Biblical truth is very important in the home. One's attitude is a healthy way of keeping your family unit strong. Putting work ahead of your family can damage relationships and reduce bonding time. This is the same for ministers as well. You can't be expected to lead a church if you're failing in leading your home. When you are homeschooling, you can teach your kids a firm foundation of faith, help them with their academics, and build a strong relationship with your children. You want to teach your children who they are, before the world teaches them who they should be. I did not homeschool my children long term. I homeschooled them during their middle years only 6th, 7th, and 8th grade. This was such a crucial point in their lives to have guidance before going to high school. This is a critical time for emotional development, developing personality traits, curiosity and study habits and making good decisions. My oldest was always two grades behind in reading, terrible hand writing, and attention issues. He would break pencils, play with his chair, desk, and talk often. We did not put him on meds for ADHD, but instead worked on naturalistic ways to help with ADHD. Some naturalistic things we did was cut out red dyes, use essential oils, increase Omega threes, cut out sugar, and find outlets for his energy. I always communicated with teachers, helped with homework, and paid for tutors. But it wasn't working. Something had to change. Homeschooling is a lifestyle choice. You are choosing to have less of a family income; therefore, less vacations and materialistic possessions. Every homeschool situation is different and I can only speak from my own experience that it was the best thing I did for my children's relationship with God and each other. We have great communication and memories because we chose to homeschool.

According to the article, how religion impacts development in young children by MEENA AZZOLLINI February 8, 2019, it states, "More frequent parent-child discussions of religion significantly improved test scores for reading. This suggests that such conversations—perhaps practiced as scripture study or religious devotionals within the home—might enhance children's literacy. Also, some forms of parental religiosity (fathers' attendance and both spouses attending semiregularly or frequently) had a positive outcome on children's approach to learning as rated by the teachers. The study found that religious solidarity among couple and communication between parent and children were associated with positive development, but religious conflict among parents was linked to negative outcomes in children."

In Ephesians 5:22-33 Paul begins building for us the family unit. He clearly lays out the role of the husband and wife in relation to Christ and his bride, the Church. In the first few verses of Ephesians 6, he'll continue to build for us the God-ordained design of the family. Families are intended to be unified, kind, loving, godly, helpful, selfless, and a witness and reflection of God.

Private Education-A private school is a school not administered or funded by the government, unlike a public school. They are also known as independent schools, non-government, privately funded, or non-state schools. They are usually funded by fees charged at their students. According to the article found on https://www. hotchkiss.org the top benefits of private school are the following:

1. Parental involvement
2. Safe Learning environment
3. Strong Sense of Community
4. Individualized Attention from teachers-Class size is smaller
5. Increased Access to Opportunities-Better books, supplies, sports, music, drama, and technology
6. Tuition Assistance and Grants
7. Higher Academic Standards-Higher graduation and college acceptance rates

Some disadvantages to private school according to https://blog.fms. org are the following:

1. Limited Resources- private schools may have different levels of funding
2. Less diversity-more than 75% of the student body is white
3. More pressure to perform

One must consider the cost, curriculum, and location of the school. I have worked at 3 different types of Private schools-Montessori, Catholic, and Mennonite preschool. What I have learned about all three is that parents make the choice and are dedicated to their child being there. Montessori was discovered by a woman by the name of Maria Montessori an Italian educator who wanted disadvantaged school children to have a quality education. Now Montessori is for the elite, advantaged children with high income whose families can afford to have their child go there. Although Montessori has an amazing philosophy of life skills Head start programs are now for the disadvantaged low-income families of today. Faith and Religion are at the fore front of the elementary Catholic School and Mennonite preschool that I've worked for. For emotional skills I had students at the Catholic school draw me a picture about how they felt while in Mass. Most of the students drew happy faces, but two of the students drew a sad face and another student drew an angry face. These were kindergarten students and I had assumed that they drew these faces because they were bored in Mass. Mass can be a bit boring for kindergarten kids who are required to sit still and be quiet for a long period of time. When asked why they drew those faces they said it was because they were sad/mad of the visuals of Jesus dying on the cross. This was an aha moment for me, I should not assume as to why someone may feel the way they feel. I also witnessed an amazing miracle at this Catholic school. The school owed the Diocese 500,000 dollars for the doors to remain open. Teachers got layoff notices. The parents, students, and teachers worked hard to make this not happen. We all collaborated on fundraisers. We had a very pregnant mom in the kitchen make tamales. I believe we made 17, 000 off tamale sales. We had yard sales, students were making bracelets to sell, we had a Cinco de mayo fundraiser where we made 70,000. We made 250,000 dollars in two months. An anonymous donner came in to close the gap. The doors at this school stayed open. Often parents are blaming the teachers for not doing their job or teachers are upset with parents for not doing their job. What an amazing experience to see parents and teachers come together. The dedication of these parents and teachers inspired me.

At the Mennonite preschool/after school program that I work at I have found the staff and children that I work with phenomenal. I am always inspired and learning. The students make my heart happy for their love of the Lord. Seeing the kids faces light up as they enter the school is my favorite part of the day. There long tight hugs allow me the moments of feeling God's love. There is a special work family there that I love dearly and enjoy being around.

Families who see faith as more important than academics often want their children to come to a faith based private school. The benefits I see here are teachers who strive to set Christ like examples and morals. Teachers who practice the fruits of the spirit of Love, Joy, Peace, Patience, goodness, kindness, and self-control. Teachers who will read Bible stories and worship with the students. Although private school cost money I also believe you get what you pay for. Smaller class sizes and more one on one attention for extra support. For some families, a faith institution or spiritual practice group serves the same function as a close-knit neighborhood, providing friendship, a social life, mutual aid, social services, support, counseling, and education, along with worship service, celebrations, and/or spiritual guidance.

JESUS FOLLOWERS LED
THE MODERN EDUCATION
REVOLUTION

O ne of my favorite quotes is from President Theodore Roosevelt "A thorough knowledge of the Bible is worth more than a college education." We live in a world today where I see the dangers of a public school and university education. Public schools and colleges teach principles opposed to Christianity. Max Planck said, "It was not by accident that the greatest thinkers of all ages were deeply religious souls." Education during the common Era points to Jesus. Even if you haven't attended a university, you've experienced the impact of Jesus followers at some point in your education. Christians have been educational innovators. A Jesus follower at some point in history had shaped every aspect of our education.

Most of this section is found in the book <u>Person of Interest-Why Jesus Still Matters In a World That Rejects The Bible </u>by J. Warner Wallace.

> The first modern universities were established in Bologna, Oxford, and Paris. All were founded by Jesus followers. The University of Bologna (established in 1088 CE) still bears the motto, "St. Peter is everywhere the father of the law, Bologna is its mother." Oxford University (founded in 1096 CE) has a motto that includes the opening words to Psalm 27 NIV: "The Lord is my light." The University of Paris (founded in 1150 CE) emerged from cathedral schools of Norte Dame

and became "the most celebrated teaching centre of all Christendom." These Three Schools were so influential that they gave birth to other universities during the scientific revolution of the 16th and 17th century. Those universities became monasteries and cathedral schools that were inspired by Jesus. Jesus followers had an overwhelming impact on the history of education and establishing modern universities is only part of the story.

If you were asked to read books as part of your education (at the primary, secondary, or university level), you can thank Johannes Gutenberg (C. 1400-1468 CE), devoted Jesus follower and the creator of the printing press.

If you benefited from an organized, public educational system in your community, you can thank Johannes Begenhagen (1485-1558 CE), a Jesus follower who pioneered the organization of schools, Philipp Melanchthon (1497-1560 CE), a theologian who was also a pioneer of public education, Jon Comenius (1592-1670 CE), a Moravian Brethren bishop (considered the "father of modern education") who advocated for universal education; and Jean-Baptiste de La Salle (1651-1719 CE), a French priest who promoted compulsory education and spent much of his life education the poor.

If you had access to an education as a child, you can thank Martin Luther (1483-1546 CE), the German theologian and religious reformer who argued for universal education and literacy for children; John Calvin (1509-1564 CE), the French theologian and reformer who advocated for "a system of elementary education in the vernacular for all, including reading, writing, arithmetic, grammar, and religion; and Friedrich Froebel (1782-1852 CE), the son of a Lutheran pastor who is known as the "father of Kindergarten education."

If you found satisfaction in advancing from one grade to the next, you can thank Johann Sturm (1507-1589 CE), the Lutheran layman who introduced the notion of grade levels to motivate students to study so they could earn the reward of advancing to the next level.

If you had access to an education as a person with disabilities, you can thank Charles- Michel de l'Epee (1712-1789 CE), the ordained priest (called the "father of education for the deaf") who developed sign language for use in schools, Laurent Marie Clerc (1785- 1869 CE), the committed Christ follower who brough sign language to the United States; Thomas Hopkins Gallaudet (1787-1851 CE), the congregational clergyman who opened the first school for the deaf in the United States, or Louis Braille (1809-1852 CE), the Catholic priest (known as the "father or education for the blind") who developed a system of reading and writing for the blind and visually impaired.

If you received an education in a foreign land, you can thank the inspiration of Frank Laubach (1884-1970 CE), a Methodist missionary (known as "the apostle to the illiterates") who traveled to more than 100 countries, developed primers in 313 languages, and created a literacy program that has been used to teach nearly 60 million people to read in their own language.

Jesus matters to the history of education. Jesus followers laid the foundation for schools as we know them today, from kindergarten to universities. Christan contributed to the progress of education and founded more universities and colleges than all their religious predecessors. Even though Hindus had a 2,300 to 1500-year advantage, Jews had a 2,000- to 1,800-year lead, and Buddhist and Zoroastrians had a 600-year head start, Christians established more universities than all other groups combined by a magnitude of ten to one. And universities founded by Christians STILL dominate the educational landscape.

Just imagine for a moment that you want your child to go to the best University in the world. After an internet search you have come up with a list of the top Universities. The following is a list of the best ranked Universities:

Harvard University

Massachusetts Institute of Technology

Standford University

University of Cambridge

University of Oxford

Columbia University

Princeton University

University of California, Berkeley

University of Pennsylvania

University of Chicago

Yale University

University of Paris (Sorbonne)

University of Michigan

This is an exceptional list and it represents the finest in the world. Your child would be fortunate to attend any of these schools, but would you be surprised to learn that all of them were founded by Christians, most for the purpose of teaching Christian principles? It's true. If you were to visit these universities and examine the original buildings and founding charters you would learn that Jesus inspired the creation of the buildings. You could see the historical truth of Jesus of Nazareth. The original buildings on these campuses typically include chapels and halls that display either images of Jesus or passages from the New Testament. The original charters also reveal truths about Jesus, based on the stated purposes of each university. This is not only shown in the top 15 universities but also the top 50 universities on earth showing the truths of Jesus. Most of the founders of the world's top fifty universities were devout Christians who regularly preached and wrote about Jesus. Even though many of these schools have abandoned their Christian identity, their building and charters tell a different story, unanimously pointing back to the man who inspired their creation. Any effort to remove Jesus from history would also require the destruction or reconstruction of the world's leading universities. No other historical figure is better represented in university buildings, and bylaws, and founding charters.

Colleges today in 2023 are the opposite of what it was intended to be. The woke-left agenda is taking over our colleges. It's become an institution on teaching students what to think instead of how to think. It's focused on turning students into victims, anti-American sympathizers and social-justice warriors by graduation. In the article, Why I'm leaving college and choosing education over indoctrination by the New York Post by author CJ Pearson states, "I no longer have any interest in paying to be told my blackness is a disability and all white people are evil. And asked what my pronouns are when-at least in my opinion-it should be clear as day." The article goes on to say, "Stanford University shamelessly embrace the absurd: labeling words such as 'American' and 'grandfather' racist and harmful. It allows Rutgers University to declare a war on grammar-casting it aside as racist in an effort to 'stand with and respond to' the Black Lives Matter movement. And it's why places like Berkely-once heralded as bastion of free speech-have become symbolic of everything wrong with higher education today" (CJ Pearson, 2023). Parents who are paying for tuition might want to take note, and see what their hard-earned money is paying for.

Equality is recognized in the Declaration of Independence. "All men are created equal, endowed by their creator with certain unalienable Rights." Equality recognizes equal origins. Equity is about equal outcomes. That's very different. It's not even biblical. Everyone is made in God's image (equal origins), but Jesus said we don't receive equal abilities. With different levels of abilities, different levels of outcomes are expected (Matthew 25:14-30). Based on what we make of what we're given, God then distributes different levels of rewards (Luke 19). We are made in Gods image, but we are responsible for the outcomes. One could have a gift or talent, but if you get lazy and don't put it to use what good is your talent or gift. What we are seeing now in equity is the claim that the unfair treatment of previous generations entitles one to special consideration today as an adult. Equity sounds good on the surface, but it takes a biblical idea, hollows it out, and redefines it. The version of equity taught in public schools maintains the concept of fairness, but redefines what is fair according to human standards rather than God's law. According to the article, Understanding Educational Equity: What it is and why it should be rejected by Josh Mulvihill, "It is essential to recognize that equity is an ideology that has set aside classic liberal education ideals in favor of a new progressive creed. This creed, often know as 'critical race theory,' diminishes individual identity in favor of group identities based on gender, race, sexuality, and religion. It understands identity groups to be in constant conflict with one another and believes justice involves taking power from the oppressor groups and giving it to the oppressed. It holds this to be the key to ushering in the long-awaited educational utopia that will fix academic problems." (Josh Mulvihill). According to the Bible, this is a distorted version of equity. As a result, it is unjust and discriminatory because it is based on skin color, gender, sexual orientation, or religion. Equity must have a standard of good and bad and right and wrong. The problem is that public schools have ono objective foundation for morality. God's law, the Ten Commandments, was removed from public schools in the 1960s. Public schools are indoctrinating children with a secular view of morality such as the term equity, white privilege, systemic racism, and anti-bias training. In chapter 10 of the child development college textbook Child, Family, and Community Family-Centered Early Care and Education by Janet Gonzalez-Mena 7th Edition states the following, "Start by modeling anti-bias behaviors. Become aware that the white able-bodied male is a privilege group." (Janet Gonzales-Mena, P. 234). Isn't this quote in a child development textbook being biased? You can see the indoctrination in our curriculum. White privilege tells us that we must be racist because we are white. White privilege tells you that you are only successful because of the color of your skin. In chapter 10 of the child development college textbook Child, Family, and Community Family-Centered Early Care and Education by Janet Gonzalez-Mena 7th Edition states the following, "It is only fair that both genders be allowed and indeed encouraged to expand beyond the limits of narrow gender roles. It is not fair to exclude someone from playing because of skin color, gender, or ability." (Janet Gonzales-Mena, P. 234). The above quote says both genders as in two not all genders as in more than two or to include transgender. Men compete in men's sports and woman compete in woman sports. Right now, I'm thinking of Riley Gaines who is speaking out against Lia Thomas. Lia Thomas is a born male claiming to be female swimming in a woman's sport. A male changing in the locker room with girls. A male competing against woman. How is this fair? How is this not sexual misconduct? The female athletes are discriminated against because of their sex. As shown in the above child development college textbook quote and in our society, we are now to include transgenders in sports. If we are a society who wants woman rights, how is it so bluntly obvious that they are taking those rights away? So much contradictory by our secular world today. The best way to promote unity is to promote truth.

Skeptics sometimes claim Christians haven't historically advanced the gospel with a well-reasoned, educated approach, but have instead acted violently to force people to convert to Christianity. Have people behaved violently under the Christian banner? Yes. Does the Christian worldview as taught by Jesus endorse this approach? No. Christianity grew exponentially in the earliest centuries of the Common Era, when followers of Jesus were powerless, persecuted, and pursued. They simply obeyed the counterintuitive commands of their Master to love their enemies (Matthew 5:44), turn the other cheek (Matthew 5:39), and to pray for those who abused them (Luke 6:28). Christianity grew not as a result of violence, but as Christ follower advanced education across the globe.

Christ followers celebrated the Life of the Mind. Jesus encourages his followers to worship God with their intellectual and rational abilities. When a skeptical Jewish Pharisee (a sect of Jewish believes that strictly observed the Jewish traditions and laws asked Jesus, "Teacher, which is the greatest command in the Law?" Jesus replies, "You shall love the Lord our God with all your heart and with all your soul and with all your mind" (Matthew 22:36-37 ESV)

Christ followers collected and protected knowledge. The early Christians were also thinkers who studied the Scriptures as the "Word of God" and eventually became known "along with their Jewish predecessors) as "People of the Book." Christians and Jews were students of Scripture. Moses started this educational emphasis many centuries earlier: "These words that I command you today shall be on your heart. You shall teach them diligently to your children, and shall talk of them when you sit in your house, and when you walk by the way, and when you lie down, and when you rise" (Deuteronomy 6:6-7 ESV) Christians continued this tradition of education. Paul reiterated this emphasis in a letter to his disciple

Timothy: "All Scripture is God-breathed and is useful for teaching, correcting and training in righteousness" (2 Timothy 3:16 NIV).

Christ followers were called to make disciples. From start to finish, Jesus and his follower held education in high regard. Jesus's last words to his disciple made this clear: "All authority in heaven and on earth has been given to me. Go therefore and make disciples of all nations, baptizing them in the name of the Father and of the Son and of the Holy Spirit, teaching them to observe all that I have commanded you. And behold, I am with you always, to the end of the age" (Matthew 28:18-20 ESV). Jesus commanded his follower to make disciples, and this required them to become teachers of the Word.

Christ followers embraced a "teaching" Culture. Jesus was both a learner and a teacher. As a child he sat at the feet of instructors in the temple (Luke 2:46), and he later spent his entire ministry teaching his disciples. He prepared his students and sent them to share the truth with others and even used teaching imagery in his illustrations and sermons: "A disciple is not above his teacher, but everyone when he is fully trained will be like his teacher" (Luke 6:40 ESV). Paul later affirmed the duty to educate the community of saints: "let the word of Christ dwell in your richly, teaching and admonishing one another in all wisdom" (Colossians 3:16 ESV).

Christ followers embraced their responsibility to learn the truth. Early Christians understood their personal responsibility as students. They were individually transformed by learning the truth and by using their minds to continually evaluate the will of God as it was described in the Book: "Do not be conformed to this world, but be transformed by the renewals of your mind, that by testing you may discern what is the will of God, what is good and acceptable and perfect." (Romans 12:2 ESV).

Christ followers educated the world to share the gospel. Jesus followers took seriously the command to "go therefore and make disciples" (Mathew 28:19 ESV). They branched out into the world and immediately encountered a significant obstacle: discipleship was dependent on the Book, but not every new people group could read. Some groups didn't even possess an alphabet of their own. This didn't stop Christian missionaries.

WHAT ABOUT COLLEGES NOW?

The higher education system indoctrinates America's youth. Most of the professors are leftist. "A poll conducted of Ivy League professors and administrators at liberal arts and social science faculties showed that 84 percent voted for Al Gore in 2000, as opposed to 9 percent for George W. Bush. Fifty-seven percent identified themselves as Democrats while only 3 percent identified themselves as Republicans" (Shapiro). As a conservative professor I have seen firsthand the leftist brainwashing occurring on campus on a daily basis. Why should I teach a point of view I don't agree with. Professors that identify with leftist politics rarely misses an opportunity to plant those leftist ideas in the minds of their students. The ideas extend only from the left to the far left. Students aren't likely to get a well-rounded view of the world. Those that protest against leftist thought are frightened into submission. It is professional suicide to engage in free expression. Go woke or go broke. You become the person in your department that everyone hates. "The Democrats running the universities don't separate politics and teaching. In fact, the Democratic party platform provides a great description of the material professors shove down the throats of their captive audiences." (Shapiro). "Republicans are not welcome on campus. Conservatives are not even allowed to speak at college graduations. The Center for the Study of Popular Culture researched the political views of graduation speakers over a ten-year period, covering thirty-two colleges, including all lvy League schools. Speakers with liberal ideas outnumbered speakers with conservative ideas by a margin of 226-15. Twenty-two of the thirty-two schools surveyed did not invite a single conservative to speak; during the same period, they invited 173 liberals. When

UCLA invited First Lady Laura Bush to speak of the Graduate School of Education and Information Studies commencement, everyone spiraled. Meanwhile, leftists are welcomed with open arms." (Shapiro).

The foundation of universities was once the Christian faith, not anymore. "Classes on Marxism exist at major universities across the country. The University of California at Santa Barbara offers 'Black Marxism.' Rutgers University offers 'Marxist Literary Theory.' University of California at Riverside offers a Marxist Studies minor." Universities were founded on Christian principles as discussed earlier. Marx seek to replace the Christian worldview with a vile substitute. Christians are wise to reject it. "As Dinesh D'Souza described in his book, liberal Education, 'Most American universities have diluted or displaced their core curriculum in the great works of Western civilization to make room for new course requirements stressing non-Western cultures, Afro-American studies, Women's studies... professors who are viewed as champions of minority interest...are permitted overtly ideological scholarship, and are immune from criticism even when they make excessive or outlandish claims with racial connotations." (Shapiro). "Professor Noel Ignatiev of Harvard University identifies himself as an 'abolitionist' seeking to abolish whiteness. White people must commit suicide as whites in order to ...change from the miserable, petulant, subordinated creatures they are now into freely associated, fully developed human subjects. Ignatiev also attacked the police force." (Shapiro). If more people came from the Christian mind set of one race one blood we would solve our racial issue as racism is a sin issue.

I don't think that students of the Christian faith and their parents who pay for these colleges would approve of the list of anti-Christian classes being taught in regards to sex. Here are just of few of many-This extensive list can be found in Ben Shapiro's book called Brainwashed.

UCLA: M101A-Lesbian and Gay Literature before Stonewall; M101 B-Lesbian and Gay Literature after Stonewall

California State University at Northridge: Erotic Literature, Male Sexuality, Gay Literature, and Lesbian Literature and Poetry

University Of Michigan: How to be Gay: Male Homosexuality and Initiation.

Ben Shapiro's book Brainwashed also gives names and locations of professors who teach and advocate for pornography, bondage, sex with children and animals and yet are not fired because it is considered an art form. Yet professors who are conservative or Christian are seen as the enemy. There is a war on God that is very strong in colleges. They wish to tear down biblical morality and replace it with a morality of their own choosing. It is a degraded morality they seek to promote. Without God, there is no right and wrong, no good and bad. Anything goes. Life itself loses value, and with that loss of value comes a loss of society strength. A Professor in Ben Shapiros book Brainwashed announce in their classrooms that there is no God, Jesus is half deranged. Another professor states our society should return to Pagan worship.

"Patrick Henry University, in Virginia, was denied accreditation by the American Academy of Liberal Education because it teaches creationism. Despite meeting all the criterion for accreditation and openly stating that it is a Christian college, the AALE dismissed its accreditation. University President Mike Farris calls the ruling "discrimination on the basis of viewpoint and ideology," and states that the AALE 'wants to force us to teach what they want us to teach' and he's right. If you don't teach it the liberal way, the liberal education establishment will shut you down." (Shapiro). I was just thinking about a local Christian College in the area the ministry program was shut down. Let that sink in for a moment. A CHRISTAIN COLLEGE WITH NO MINISTRY PROGRAM. Things that make you go HMMM. Professors are allowed to teach homosexuality, Marxism (a secular religion), and anti-Americanism, but mention God and you're out of a job. I have personal experience in this, being a Christian at a secular college is no joke, you stick out, you get less classes. I honestly feel I have been discriminated against based on my faith, but what else can I do but write this book and tell my story. Prove and show that others are not alone. Here's another story to illustrate my point.

"The receivers' coach for Nebraska's football team, Ron Brown, was interviewed in 2002 for the position of head coach at Stanford. Brown has a stellar record in his seventeen years at Nebraska: in that time, twenty-six of his pupils have gone on to play in the National Football League. Brown is black. It seems he would have fit perfectly into the system. There was only one problem: Brown is a religious Christian. And that was the deal-breaker. The assistant athletic director at Stanford, Alan Glenn, said that Brown's religion 'was something that had to be considered. We're a very diverse community with a diverse alumnus. Anything that would stand out that much is something that has to be looked at.' In specific, it was Brown's commitment to the biblical ban on homosexuality that Stanford found objectionable. As Brown described the discrimination against him, 'If I'd been discriminated against for being black, they never would have told me that. They had no problem telling me it was because of my Christian beliefs. Brown's story isn't unusual. Christians are turned away from university jobs and ridiculed in the classroom for their religious views." (Shapiro)

There are other stories of professors and students who become the victim of religious discrimination in the hands of administration told in Ben Shapiros booked called Brainwashed.

Higher education undermines religion. Professors wish for religion to be undermined. Professors openly proclaim their atheism. They discard organized religion as foolishness. They teach that science and religion conflict with one another. The universities themselves discriminate against religious Christians and Jews. They promote abortion, LGBTQ, Racism. God is no longer welcomed on campus.

JESUS CHRIST HAS NOT JUST AFFECTED EDUCATION

Ancient people groups often adopted the god(s) of their parents and the culture where they were raised, but this was not true for the young Christian movement. Instead, Christianity emerged in a largely Jewish and pagan culture that was hostile to the claims of Christianity. New believers did not become Christian because Christianity was the default religion of the time. The same can be said for many new believers today. Some of us may have adopted the religion of our parents, but this does not explain the explosive historic growth of Christianity. The next few paragraphs I will go over the impact Jesus has made globally from books, movies art, science, and music.

Even if we burned all Bibles, we would be able to know about Jesus Christ. The voices of non-Christians who dislike Jesus can be heard on the pages of historical manuscripts. These ancient Roman and Jewish voices were clearly hostile to Christianity. People who disliked Jesus can still tell you the life of Jesus, his ministry, his followers, the titles he had, his trial, his crucifixion, and his resurrection. All coming from the mouths of non-Christian.

Jesus dominates bookshelves such as History of the Church by Eusebius (c.330 CE), The Pilgrim's Progress by John Bunyan (1678 CE), The Cost of Discipleship by Dietrich Bonhoeffer (1937 CE), or Mere Christianity by C.S Lewis (1952 CE). These are just to name a few of many. The global database reveals that Jesus is still the subject of more books than anyone else. There are 109,000,000 books that speak about Jesus. In second place is George Washington at 58,400,000 (Google Books- https://books. google.com/)

Jesus became the focus of writers who were inspired by Jesus's impact on cultures. According to the book <u>A Person of Interest</u> by J. Warner Wallace, "Some of the earliest attempts to create motion pictures featured the life and activity of Jesus. In 1897 Albert Kirchner filmed La Passion du Christ, while Mark Klaw and Abraham Erlanger created The Horitz Passion Play. These primitive films started an explosion of cinematic activity depicting the life of Jesus" (Wallace). Films about Jesus continue today. Cecil B. DeMille directed The King of Kins (1927 version), Martin Scorsese directed The Last Temptation of Christ, Mel Gibson directed The Passion of the Christ and Andrew Lloyed Webber scored Jesus Christ Superstar. Jesus matters to authors, writers, creators, and screenwriters in the modern era.

Jesus is also seen in architecture, landscape, statues, and art. Early centuries, early middle-Middle Ages, renaissance, and modern era all depict art work that tells the story of Jesus. If Mark's gospel was destroyed it could be reconstructed or the earliest Christian art. Every important detail about the life and ministry of Jesus as described in the gospel of Mark has been painted or sculpted by inspired artist in the earliest centuries of the Common Era. If the New Testament manuscripts were gone you would be able to retell the events of Jesus, unless those priceless works of art were destroyed to.

"Christianity had an oversized impact on science. Whatever your fascination with science, your area of interest was probably founded by a Christian who worked during the scientific revolution. When Christians established modern universities, they ignited the progress of science. If you did an online search, you would find that Jesus followers dominated the sciences. Christians in the Common Era contributed to physical sciences, medicine, mathematics, physics, and philosophy. Hospitals, as we know them today, emerged from the efforts of Christ followers. Darwin changed the religious land scape of science. His theory of evolution eliminated the need for God" (J. Warner Wallace). As Richard Dawkins wrote, "Darwin made it possible to become an intellectually fulfilled atheist." You would think that the number of Jesus followers in science would decrease once naturalistic evolution replaced God as an explanation. But nope, that did not happen. "Jesus followers also dominated the late modern (even post-Darwin) era with 450 honorees. Jesus followers didn't simply contribute to the sciences, they founded and led the sciences. Most Nobel prize winners have, in fact, been Jesus followers" (J. Warner Wallace).

Jesus is in the earliest of hymns to the billboard music of today. Carrie Underwood sang, "Jesus, Take the Wheel. Kenya West sang "Jesus Walks," and Elvis Presly sang "Reach out to Jesus." This is just to name a few of the many, many songs written about Jesus. "Today, from countless paintings, statues, and buildings, from literature and history, from personality and institution, from profanity, popular song, and entertainment media, from confession and controversy, from legend and ritual-Jesus stands quietly at the center of the contemporary world, as he himself predicted. (Dallas Willard).

COMMUNITY OUTREACH PROGRAMS THAT HELP CHILDREN AND FAMILIES

In Child development Ecology class one of the student learning outcomes focuses on Community outreach. I live in the Fresno County area of California and work in a city that is in Tulare County. This section of the paper focuses on community outreach programs in those two areas. The information about each community outreach was found on their websites.

Did you know that most community outreach programs are founded on the principles of faith? Here are some examples just to name a few:

Salvation Army- The Salvation Army, an international movement, is an evangelical part of the universal Christian Church. Its message is based on the Bible. Its ministry is motivated by the love of God. Its mission is to preach the gospel of Jesus Christ and to meet human needs in His name without discrimination.

My sons and I have volunteered the last five years for bellringing around Christmas time. The money donated 90% goes into to the community often buying school supplies and backpacks for kids amongst other things. We always have a good time drinking our hot chocolate and listing to Christmas music as we ring the bells and talk to the people in our community. https://www.salvationarmy.org/

KCAPS (Kingsburg Community Assistance Programs and Services)- This is much more than a thrift store or food bank. They are a ministry seeking to help the whole person. They seek to follow the Lord's instruction to "Love your Neighbor" Through our actions. Address specific needs such as food, clothing, housing, spiritual guidance, education, and job skills in the spirit of love and servanthood. http://kcaps.net/

Love Inc -Every year, Love INC of Tulare County connects its partner church volunteers to over 500 families in their community. Together they can not only meet over 1,000 needs, but meet each person where they are at. Caring for them holistically, the neighbors are met with dignity and respect, while our partner churches are free to focus on serving according to their strengths. As a result, lives our transformed, churches are transformed, and communities are transformed.

This is similar to KCAPS as it helps provide basic needs as well. Here is story found on the LOVE INC website: Two years ago, Alex was homeless with two children in foster care. Ready to work toward the stable, positive environment his family needed, he moved across the country, and reached out to LOVE INC of Merced, CA for help. Church volunteers delivered furniture to his home. A simple start to an ongoing relationship. Soon he began volunteering in their furniture ministry. https://www.loveinc.org/

FCA (Fellowship of Christian Athletes)-A community working to see the world transformed by Jesus Christ through the influence of coaches and athletes. This organization desires to see every coach and athlete enter a growing relationship with Jesus Christ and his church. They seek to make disciples through our strategy of engaging equipping and empowering coaches and athletes to know and grow in Christ and lead others to do the same. FCA camps are a time of "inspiration and perspiration" for athletes and coaches who want to reach their potential through comprehensive athletic, spiritual and leadership training. As a competitor, your worth and identity can be found in something more than your sport. Learn how God can take you from performing for the things of this world to finding a greater purpose in him. Here you will discover your greater potential, greater promise, greater performance and greater purpose as a coach or athlete. https://www.fca.org/

Goodwill- Goodwill helps people improve their lives by assisting individuals to find job and grow their careers. In 2022, Goodwill served over 2 million individuals worldwide and helped more than

128,998 people train for careers in industries such as banking, IT and health care, to name a few, and get the supportive services they needed to be successful such as English language training, additional education, and access to transportation and child care. Goodwill works to enhance people's dignity and quality of life by strengthening their communities, eliminating their barriers to opportunity, and helping them reach their full potential through learning and the power of work. Goodwill was founded in Boston Reverend Edgar J. Helms, a Methodist minister and early social innovator. Helms created the Goodwill philosophy of "not charity, but a chance" when he collected used household goods and clothing in wealthier areas of the city, then trained and hired people who were poor to mend and repair the used goods. The goods were then sold or given to the people who repaired them. 120 years later, Goodwill remains a household name leading nonprofit provider of educational workforce-related services. https://www.goodwill.org/

Bethlehem Center in Visalia, Ca-The Bethlehem Center is one of the only dining halls that provides hot food prepared daily. Also providing Visalia's needy families of the community with pantry food boxes. The Bethlehem Center is one of few places that needy families can turn to in time of need; Reaching out to those without a house to live in, by offering clothing to its impoverished population. Through the help of volunteers and everyday people from the community, the Bethlehem Center is able to help. The Bethlehem Center is a mission of <u>Good Shepherd Catholic Parish</u> in Visalia dedicated to provide food clothing to those in need in an atmosphere of dignity and respect. "Feed the hungry! Help those in trouble! Then your light will shine out form the darkness, and the darkness around you shall be as bright as day. And the Lord will guide you continually, and satisfy you with all good things, and keep you healthy to; and you will be like a well-watered garden, like an ever-flowing spring. (Isaiah 58:10-11) https://bethlehemcenters.org/

Mennonite Disaster Relief- The goal is to restore hope for survivors of disaster. This is done by recruiting, organizing and empowering volunteers to repair and rebuild the homes of those impacted by disasters in Canada and the U.S. They strive to be the hands and feet of Jesus to those affected by disasters. For generations Mennonites and other Anabaptist groups, mutual aid has been an informal practice expressing their faith in the day-to-day actions of caring for one another. Through spontaneous gesture of assistance, such as the well-known barn raising, the Anabaptists put their faith into action when fellow church members or neighbors faced calamity. http://mds.org

Lighthouse- "Lighthouse Counseling and Family Resource Center was formed in 1996 as part of the Western Placer Unified School District (WPUSD) serving families with children attending WPUSD. In 2005, Lighthouse became a separate 501c3 non-profit which allowed Lighthouse to expand its operations and serve more families in the Lincoln area. Continually expanding its reach across Placer County, today Lighthouse is a full-service Counseling and Family Resource Center serving approximately 4,000 Placer County residents each year. Lighthouse's reputation for providing quality services to individuals and families in need continues to grow and over time has received numerous awards. In 2010, 2012, 2013, 2017, 2018, 2019, 2020 and 2022 Lighthouse won the "Nonprofit of the Year" award by the Lincoln Chamber of Commerce. In 2012, 2014 and 2015 Lighthouse won "Best in Collaboration Award" from the Placer Collaborative Network. In 2013, Lighthouse was awarded "Best of the Best" from the Lincoln News Messenger in the categories of Best Overall Nonprofit and Best Customer Service. In 2014, Lighthouse was honored to receive five awards for "Best of the Best" by the Lincoln News Messenger. The five awards included Best Non-Profit, Best Customer Service, Best Office Staff, Best Website and Best Volunteers. In 2015, we won "Best of the Best" for Best Website and Best Place to Work. Lighthouse was a 2017 finalist for the Rocklin Chamber of Commerce in the categories of "Certified Smile Maker Award" and "Community Service Organization of the Year." Our Executive Director was also nominated as "Business Person of the Year." In 2020, Lighthouse again won "Nonprofit of the Year" award by the Lincoln News Messenger. In 2021, Lighthouse was named California Nonprofit of the Year. Over the years, Lighthouse has received multiple

Certificates of Recognition from Senator Ted Gaines, Assembly Member Kevin Kiley, U.S. Congressman Tom McClintock, and the Lincoln Community Foundation. Overall, Lighthouse enjoys a very positive reputation for providing quality, professional, caring, and collaborative services within Placer County. Lighthouse Core Values are the following:

> FAMILY: We value the structure, internal relationships, and uniqueness of each family.

> COMPASSION: We value the physical and emotional health and mental well-being of each youth, adult, and family in our community.

> CHARACTER: We believe in the inherent goodness of all youth, adults, and families and in their ability to make healthy choices and positive change.

> DEDICATION: We value our board and staff commitment to timely intervention and programming that address youth and families in need or in crisis in our community.

> COMMUNITY: We value our agency's internal relationships and collaborations with partner agencies and the community in order to provide proficient services.

> PROFESSIONALISM: We are committed to maintaining the highest levels of professionalism applying principles of altruism, excellence, caring, ethics, respect, honest communication, and accountability, and by working together with other professionals to achieve optimal health and wellness for the people we serve. https://lighthousefrc.org/about-us/

Welcome Home Outreach-I have had the amazing opportunity to volunteer with Welcome home Outreach. This is not a local outreach program, but one I am passionate about. Welcome Home Outreach Ministries has been sharing the love of Jesus Christ in the Vicente Guerrero region of Baja California Norte, Mexico. God's blessing has grown the ministry from a bus, to a tent, to the present facility that is over half a city block. For many years Welcome Home served as an orphanage. It now continues to serve families and children by providing free, loving Christian daycare to preschool-aged children of indigent farm workers. Welcome Home also shares Christ's love by:

House building and house repairs for needy families, in cooperation with visiting missions' teams who provide funding and labor.

Sharing resources with individuals and families as needs arise. This might include food bags, money and transportation for medical needs, and even a hot meal to individuals who show up on; our doorstep. According to how God provide an directs, we give and serve in HIS NAME. https://welcomehomeoutreach.org/

Being able to build a home for a family who lives on dirt and has tarp and pallets as their living structure is such a humbling experience. To have no running water, no electricity, no plumbing, and little food and yet a very happy family with strong work ethics makes me realize how little you need to be happy. It really puts into perspective your wants vs your needs.

The following are not faith based, but good community programs:

Habitat for Humanity-Habitat for Humanity is a global nonprofit housing organization working in local communities across all 50 states in the U.S. and in approximately 70 countries. Habitat's vision is of a world where everyone has a decent place to live. Habitat works toward our vision building strength, stability, and self-reliance in partnership with families in need of decent and affordable housing. Habitat homeowners help build their own homes alongside volunteers and pay an affordable mortgage. By partnering with Habitat, families and communities transform their lives with the incredible effects of safe and affordable shelter, including improvement in health, safety, child development, economic opportunity, and educational achievement. https://www.habitat.org/

WIC (Woman's Infants, and Children)-If you are pregnant, have just had a baby, are breastfeeding, or have a child under the age of five, and you meet the income guidelines, you might be eligible for the women, Infants, and Children program. Families with children under five who were previously on Healthy Families and now have Medi-Cal may be eligible for WIC. WIC is designed to help pregnant women, new mothers, and young children eat well and stay healthy. WIC provides nutrition education, breastfeeding support, and referrals to health care and social services. The WIC card can be used to by nutritious foods at many local stores. https://www.cdph.ca.gov/Programs/CFH/DWICSN/Pages/Program-Landing1.aspx

Government Assistance-As the official benefits website of the U.S government, our mission is to increase citizen access to benefit information, while reducing the expense and difficulty of interacting with the government. Medical, cash aid, food stamps, in home supportive services, disaster Relief, mental health help, transportation, help with utilities just to name a few that is offered. https://www.mybenefitscalwin.org/#/home

Care pregnancy center located in Tulare and Visalia-This center offers Confidential services, free pregnancy testing, compassionate support, parenting/birthing classes, ultra sounds, items for the baby such as clothes, bottles, diapers, car seats and much more. They also offer information on abortion https://carepregnancycenter.com/

They really SLOW the process down and give you ALL information. This gives you the opportunity to really think about your decision and the consequences it could have mentally or physically on your body. Some of the staff there are Christian. You might think, what in the world would a Christian do at an organization that performs murders. Then I got to thinking if you are determined to end a life what better person to have next to you than a compassionate Christian that will guide you through the guilt and shame and teaches Jesus's love of Forgiveness, Grace, and Mercy.

I have been told that I'm not including community outreach programs for the LGBTQ community from my superiors. My suggestion would be any church. There are tons of churches that are associated with helping with the LGBTQ community. I really could go on and on with community outreach programs, but for the sake of this paper, I'm going to stop.

HOW CHILD DEVELOPMENT IS AFFECTED BY OTHER RELIGIONS

Religion in the cultures of the Middle East:

" The Middle East is the birthplace of Judaism, Christianity, and Islam, all monotheistic religions that grew from the same tradition. Each religion used the texts from earlier groups, and so they share many rules and beliefs. For example, Islam and Judaism observe the same dietary rules and have a similar focus on religion as a foundation for civil law. All three share a tradition of prophets, from Adam and Abraham to Solomon and Joseph. Jesus is significant for both Christianity and Islam, and Muslims in addition follow the teachings of Muhammad.

Religion plays a large part in the rhythm of daily life, not only through prayer and study, but also in determining the end of the work week. Shops in different neighborhoods close down on Fridays for the Muslim holy day, Saturdays for the Jewish Sabbath, and Sundays for the Christian day of rest. Religious festivals and remembrances, like Id al-Fitr (the Festival of Fast-Breaking, celebrated at the end of Ramadan), or the Jewish Passover holiday, or Easter Sunday as determined by the Roman or Eastern Orthodox Christian churches, are all recognized as national holidays in different countries.

An awareness of God (Arabic: Allah) is exhibited in common Arabic expressions that are used throughout the region – even in Turkey and Iran, where Arabic is not the local language. A common response to "How are you?" is "Ilhamdillah!" – "Praise be to God." When expressing hope for a future event, one might say "Inshallah" – "God willing." The exclamation "Mashallah" – "What God wills!" – is often heard as an expression of delight, at the sight of a new baby, for example. While there are those for whom these phrases reflect the divine, others use them the way many English speakers use "Good-bye" (literally, "God be with ye").

Religion plays a role in national and international politics as well. Turkey has a Muslim majority, but is officially a secular nation. Other countries in the region identify themselves with a specific religion, mostly Islam. Lebanon's constitution attempted to provide for power sharing among 18 officially recognized religions, including Maronite and Orthodox Christians, Sunni and Shii Muslims, and Druze. But because the populations of the various groups grew at different rates, this system eventually became less representative of the nation as a whole and civil war broke out.

The poor relations between Israel and most of its Arab neighbors are sometimes described in terms of a perpetual religious conflict between Jews and Muslims. This reading, however, is too simplistic. Although control over important historical sites of Judaism, Christianity, and Islam is a factor in the disagreements, many of the details that stall negotiations have to do with control of land and access to water resources. Furthermore, many Palestinians who demand restitution for their property are Christian, not Muslim, and Egypt's historic treaty with Israel provides a model for how Muslim and Jewish neighbors can live peaceably.

Ethnic diversity at the crossroads of civilizations-Situated between Africa, Asia, and Europe, the Middle East has been a crossroads for traders, travelers, and empire builders for thousands of years. Africans, Central Asians, and Celts have all added to the ethnic mix. Major ethnic groups in the Middle East today include Arabs, Iranians (also known as Persians), Turks, Jews, Kurds, Berbers, Armenians, Nubians, Azeris, and Greeks.

Kurdish refugees in northern Iraq-Most of the countries in this region are multiethnic. But even as diversity enhances the cultural richness of a society, it unfortunately may also lead to political conflict. The Kurds, for example, do not have their own nation-state, but are instead spread across Turkey, Iraq, Iran, and Syria. Their political and military attempts to create an autonomous Kurdistan have been strongly resisted by those states.

Many languages, three families-The multiplicity of languages spoken in the Middle East reflects its ethnic diversity. Most of these languages come from three major language "families":

Semitic (including Arabic, Hebrew, and Aramaic)

Indo-European (Kurdish, Persian, Armenian)

Turkic (Turkish, Azeri)

These language families reflect the successive migrations of different peoples into the region. A quick examination of these languages reveals the influence they have had on each other. Persian, for example, is written in Arabic script, while Turkish incorporates vocabulary words from Persian and Arabic. Arabic itself is spoken in regional dialectics that are not always mutually understood. Some ethnic and religious communities have preserved "native" languages for religious use, such as Coptic and Greek.

Culture: Family, city, and the globe-The family is an important part of culture in the Middle East, as is evident in the Arabic honorific names that are often used in preference to given names. A man may be called Ibn ("son of") followed by his father's name or Abu ("father of") followed by his child's name.

In traditional Arab societies the family unit is an extended family – cousins, grandparents, second cousins, cousins-in-law, nieces, nephews, and more – all living together. This remains true in rural areas particularly. Migration to the cities has broken up some of these extended families, and the number of people living only with their nuclear family in urban areas is increasing.

The difference between life in the village and life in the city sometimes seems to be as great or greater than the difference between living in the Middle East and living in America. Two men in Egypt, for example, may share the same language (Arabic), religion (Islam), and nationality (Egyptian), but one may live in an air-conditioned apartment building with his wife and two children and wear a suit to his government job, while the other may live in a naturally cool mud-brick house surrounded by three generations of relatives and wear a traditional robe, called a galabiya, to work a plot of land.

These differences are eroding, however, with the introduction of inexpensive cellular phone service and the ubiquity of television. Even some mud-brick houses are now equipped with satellite dishes that bring news, entertainment, and fashions not only from the capital city, but from around the world as well." (http://www.pbs.org/wgbh/globalconnections/mideast/themes/culture/#:~:text=Religion%20in%20the%20cultures%20of%20the%20Middle%20East&text=Each%20religion%20used%20the%20texts,a%20foundation%20for%20civil%20law.)

Active research on child development and religion:

https://www.mdpi.com/2077-1444/10/11/631

https://www.researchgate.net/publication/257656700 Child Development from the Perspective of Syed Shakh Ahmad Alhady

In chapter 3 of the Child Development Ecology text book Child, Family, School, Community Socialization, and support 10ᵗʰ Edition by Roberta M. Berns, it states that, "Every religion includes some beliefs that are shared by all its adherents. For example, Judaism teaches that a "good life" can be led only in a community; good Jews must always view their actions in terms of their effect on others. They believe in responsibility for others and regard charity as a virtue. Muslims give a percentage of their annual income to the poor. The ultimate goal of Buddhism is to be fully in the world and relate compassionately to others. Through their beliefs and practices, most religions provide:

1. A divine Ideology-enables individuals to comprehend events that happen to them; death, illness, financial crises, and injustices make sense if these are seen as part of a divine plan; helps fill the gap between scientific and technical knowledge and the unknown.
2. Coping Mechanism-to help individuals accept and cope crises without overwhelming psychological costs (for example,

prayer helps people feel that they are "doing something" to meet the crisis); believing can help one avoid feeling that life's catastrophes are senseless.

3. A Concept of Death-Provides structure to life (some religions preach hell for those who transgress in life on Earth and heaven for those who lead a good life); can give hope of a blissful immorality making the death of a loved one more tolerable and the thought of one's own death less terrifying.

4. Establishment of Identity-gives meaning to life; many religious activities reflect pride and celebration; religious rituals symbolize faith, honor God, or remind members of the group of their religious responsibilities; rituals may include observing holidays, saying prayers, tithing, handling sacred objects, wearing certain clothing and eating certain food or fasting (for example, Holy Communion commemorates the climactic meal of Jesus' life and sacrifice for human kind; in partaking of the holy bread and wine, the communicant partakes of Christ).

Carl Jung (1938) wrote that religion provides individuals who have a strong commitment to traditional norm and value with moral strength and behavior stability. In other words, religious people are more likely to comply with societal norms, especially if they believe that those norms are divinely sanctioned. They look upon social deviance as a form of religious deviance. This has been confirmed in research (Furrow, King, & White, 2004; Gorsuch, 1976) showing that moral behavior has consistently been related to religious commitment."

This is where I see a STRONG benefit to learning about Religion/Faith for those who are mentally ill and why I think that every mental health facility or program should include having a relationship with God to cope. But when I make that suggestion, I'm looked at as like an absurd person for even suggesting such an idea.

PAKISTAN AND THE PERSECUTION OF CHRISTIANS RIGHT NOW IN 2023

A Christian man has been sentenced to death under blasphemy laws in Pakistan. Pakistan has some of the most difficult blasphemy laws in the world. The court system and the way these are adjudicated you have somebody who's making a claim that in most cases can't be substantiated. Blasphemy can be any sort of offense that the person interprets it as, or in other words in some cases they might say "hey, I'm a Christian" and a person could say well that's blasphemy against Muhammad and the punishment in Pakistan is the death penalty, so there's no proportionality to a particular situation, so anybody can make a charge that can't be validated and its entirely subjective. On May 30th 2023 a young man 18 years of age is accused of blasphemy and nobody can quite seem to understand what it was. In America we think about our Justice right and we have all sorts of debates about whether or not Justice is being served, but the point is people have a due process, you have to have evidence, the system isn't perfect, but its' a system of justice. When you're talking about a system like Pakistan's, anybody could come up and say anything they can, make it up and in the case were talking about there's no evidence really presented. In America we have free speech. When that begins to be taken away and the words HATE SPEECH gets thrown around than you're looking at a corrupt society that is taking away your free speech. Right now, Pakistan Muslim mobs are attacking Christian churches and targets Christians. Are Christians beginning to be attacked in America too? Is there discrimination in the work place because you are

Christian? Can it get much worse for Christians in America today? What happened to the early Christians such as Perpetua and can that happen again? Christian persecution has been around since the existence of Jesus Christ. These are just a few verses on being a BOLD Christian.

Jesus died to cleans us of our sins, so we can boldly approach our God who is holy and without sin (Hebrews 4:16).

God fills us with the Holy Spirit, who is bold and courageous (1 Timothy 1:7-8). We do not have to muster courage and strength on our own. We simply submit to the Spirit of God that is within us.

God promises that nothing can separate us from his love (Romans 8:38-39). He is always with us, especially in times of crisis.

When our hearts are aligned with God in faith, he tells us to pray with boldness, expecting that our prayers will be answered (1 John 5:14).

The Spirit of God emboldens us to proclaim the gospel without fear (1 Thessalonians 2:2).

Boldness is contagious. When we are bold for Christ, enduring hardships for our faith, others are provoked to do the same (Philippians 1:14).

WHAT IS GOING ON IN ISRAEL
RIGHT NOW IN 2023

God found favor in Abraham. God even called Abraham His friend. Abraham's wife was named Sarah and together they were leaders of a large tribe. God promised Abraham that his seed (offspring) would be numbered like the sands of the seas. Sarah was getting to be really old although people lived hundreds of years back then. She began to doubt God's promise and suggested that Abraham sleep with her very attractive and younger handmaiden, Hagar. Abraham, being human and born of a sinful nature, agreed with Sarah and because he's a guy in fact did sleep with Hagar. Soon after it was realized that Hagar was pregnant with Abraham's first born, Ishmael. True to God's promise later Sarah birthed Abrahams second son, Isaac. Since the original sin, (Adam and Eve) mankind has failed, disappointed and angered God. It was not Gods will that man fail, it has and is always been about choices and free will. From Hagar came Ishmael. From Sarah came Issac. True to Gods promise, Abraham's seed became and is as the sands of the seas. However, true to there being consequences for sin, God told Abraham that he must get the sin out of the camp. Having to banish Hagar and Ishmael from the camp grieved Abraham a great deal. He loved both of his sons like any good father would. When it comes right down to it, Ishmael was born against the will of God. From that beginning Ishmael descendants have waged war against Issacs descendants. From Ishmael came the Arab Nations, the prophet Mohammed, who was a fierce warrior and writer or the Islamic Quran, which instructs followers of Muhammad that if Christians or any other faith won't convert to Islam or the Muslim faith, they're labeled as infidels and must be killed. From Isaac came the Jewish nation and eventually Judaism, Christianity and finally Jesus as a blood sacrifice for sin to all nations. This is how the Middle East has been labeled 'the cradle of civilization'. Ishmaels descendants don't believe that Jews and Christians have a right to live. That's why leaders of Iran, direct Hamas, Hezbola, ISIS and a host of other murderous Islamic terrorist organizations to attack and chant "death to Israel and death to America." This war, jihad has been going on from the beginning and will be going on when Christ appears for His second coming to wage the final war against evil. This country has been blessed because this country has been a defender of Israel and the Jews. As you can see by the siding of the youth of this nation with supporting and protesting on the behalf of terrorists, that we're only a generation away from turning our backs on Israel. They're so misguided, indoctrinated and naive that they don't understand the weight of their actions. God chose the Jews for Jesus to take on human flesh and walk among us for 33 years, ultimately becoming a blood sacrifice on the cross. This sacrifice was not just for Christians and Jews, it was for any human who would answer the call to become Christ like.

The recent deadly terrorist attacks on Israeli civilians and soldiers have not only shocked Israel but also the world. Be in prayer for all those who have been kidnapped, for those suffering from wounds and trauma, and for the families that have lost loved ones. Be in prayer for Israel's military and first responders as they meet the crisis head on. Be in prayer for the leadership as they make tough decision.

DOES RELIGION HAVE A NEGATIVE IMPACT ON CHILD DEVELOPMENT

Influence of religion on children and their rights:

'Nearly 86% of the world's population is religious, including all religions. In numerous countries, religion guides social behavior and plays a significant role in daily life, including for children.

Definition of religion-A religion is a group of beliefs and rituals, it consists of rules, stories and symbols which are adopted by the society, a group or a person. Religion may be a way of life and/or a search for answers regarding life and death.

Definition of freedom of religion. How is it protected?

Children, like adults, have the freedom to choose and practice their religion, this right being protected by article 14 of the Convention on the Rights of the Child: "States Parties shall respect the right of the child to freedom of thought, conscience and religion."

Throughout the world, certain religious minorities are restricted and cannot practice their faith. This affects children belonging to these minorities as well, who do not have access to the same schools and, once adults, will not have access to every profession. Poorly regarded by the state and society, they remain at the margins of the community. In some countries, apostasy (changing one's religion) is a crime punishable by death.

Children, the first victims of religious conflicts:

In numerous countries and on every continent, religion can be a source of conflict, and even wars. Unfortunately, children are too commonly the victims. And, unfortunately, examples abound throughout the world.

In Africa, in Nigeria religious tensions between the predominantly Muslim north and the Christian and animistic south have resulted in a large number of deaths since Christmas 2011. In Egypt, Copts are victims of discrimination and children are the first victims. Access to school, health care and employment are restricted for the Coptic minority.

Controversial and dangerous practices:

In some countries, religious extremists strongly discriminate against women and young girls. Under the Taliban regime, in Afghanistan, girls were not allowed to go to school. This ban has since been lifted, but an entire generation of girls was never even taught to read or write. In addition, the regime banned playing in the street, laughing, singing and listening to music. Even if the Taliban is no longer in power, certain customs and traditions remain. Elsewhere still, girls continue to be subjected to discriminatory laws.

All religious fundamentalism, be it Christian, Muslim, Jewish or others, endangers the children's rights, especially those of girls. Certain religious interpretations linked to ancestral traditions can be the source of violence committed against children. Let us look specifically at the cases of female genital mutilation and child marriage.

Child Marriage:

This is the union of two children or, more often, of a young girl and an adult man, sometimes much older. These marriages can be found throughout the world, but mainly in (Sub-Saharan) Africa and Southern Asia where values such as virginity and fertility of women are very important. Child marriage is not approved by any religion, even if some still use this justification.

In Islamic West Africa, the practice of "sadaka" (offering, donation in Arabic) has become a religious practice. The parents, in order to avoid Hell, give their young girl to a marabout, a religious dignitary, or a member of their family. As this is done without the consent of the young girl, this practice goes against the Quran.

Female circumcision and genital mutilation:

Female circumcision is the mutilation of the genitals of girls, during childhood, most commonly done in unsanitary conditions. Mainly situated in Africa, the majority of populations that practice female circumcision are Muslim, but the practice is also found in Christian, as well as Jewish communities. However, no religion mentions or supports this custom.

It stems rather from ancestral tradition and popular beliefs as circumcision was already practiced before the arrival of Christianity and Islam. Recently, religious leaders have publicly opposed these mutilations. For example, in Senegal and Egypt, Imams are speaking out to these populations, calling for a ban to put a stop to this dangerous and violent practice.

The consequences of female circumcision are dramatic. Young girls can die from hemorrhages and infections, be infected by HIV/AIDS, and suffer intense physical and psychological pain.

The provision of religion for children:

Religion is very important for many societies; it allows children to learn morals, and answers questions regarding life and death, relationships between people and their place in the world, and notions of good and evil. The major religions are all based on ideals of wisdom, solidarity and justice. All this is transmitted to children by their family, school and society so that they may become wise and respectful.

Support of the Rights of the Child by religious authorities:

Religious authorities can play an important role in improving the application of the Rights of the Child. As influential and respected members of their communities, religious leaders can encourage the actions and developments of the protection of children. They also possess the necessary influence to stop these practices, customs, sources of violence and discrimination against children.

Religious leaders can become leading actors in the defense of children's rights. For example, this has been the case in Afghanistan, where the promotion of education for young girls has gone through certain religious dignitaries. In Ethiopia, a week of awareness for HIV/AIDS was created by Christian and Muslim religious leaders.

Throughout the world, many religious groups promote and actively defend the Rights of the Child, such as Islamic Relief Worldwide and Secours Catholique. This is explained by the fact that the defense and protection of children is a cornerstone in the philosophies of most religions.' https://www.humanium.org/en/children-and-religions/

This link below is more on the negative impact of religion stating that religious children are mean.

https://www.theguardian.com/world/2015/nov/06/religious-children-less-altruistic-secular-kids-study

This link below is a study on Religion and child development: Evidence from the Early Childhood Longitudinal Study

https://www.sciencedirect.com/science/article/abs/pii/S0049089X07000129

VALIDITY OF THE BIBLE

T oday Americans are searching for truth. The most fundamental truth is the reality of a sovereign God. You will be equipped to articulate and defend the truth of Christianity. Starting with how do we know we can trust the Bible? What is Truth? Truth corresponds to reality. What is real is true, what is unreal is false. The Bible makes some very distinctive truth claims. It claims, that God exists. If we can use evidence to determine Christianity is true, why call it faith? God used the evidence of the gospel eyewitness accounts to capture and record the truth about Jesus. God has chosen to communicate with us through his creation, our moral conscience, all through the teachings of the Bible. Jesus claimed to be God in the flesh and that the only way for human beings to be saved is through Him (John 14:6). There is also the death and resurrection of Jesus. These claims the Bible makes either is reality or it's not. Christians believe that they do correspond to reality, meaning the Bible is true. God really exists, Jesus in not a myth, and the resurrection really happened. But how do we know this. There are so many books that address this question. To answer this, we will be looking at various authors, books and articles discussing science, archelogy, eyewitness accounts, and history.

Science-

There is a section in Ken Ham's <u>The New Answers Book 3</u> that discusses how Astronomy confirms a young universe. This section was way to sciency for me and I'm not a scientist. It discussed moon recession, comets, faint young sun paradox, rapid star aging, and spiral galaxies. The evidence from astronomy confirms that the Bible is true.

Creation Versus evolution debate is the most foundational issue facing the Church today. Many people are overwhelmed by the so-called scientific evidence that supports evolution. They must be right if they have a PHD and they say they can prove it with radiometric dating. In its creation account and genealogies, the Bible clearly reveals the earth is about 6,000 years old. We are losing a young generation in churches due to the indoctrination of Evolution. The young people have figured out if you cannot trust the Bible about the creation accounts in Genesis, how can you trust the Bible about the things that are hard to understand. "Science itself is created based on a Christian world view. If evolution were true, would there be any reason to think that the mind would be capable of rational thought. If the universe was created due to a big bang, why would we expect it to be orderly or comprehensible? If the universe is just matter in motion, then how could there be abstract laws, such as mathematics and logic, which are required for rational thinking? If any alternative to Christianity were true, then there would be no foundation for any of the things necessary for knowledge. We know that Christianity is true because, if it were not, then we couldn't know anything at all." (Ken Ham-How do we Know the Bible is True?). Remember all knowledge is in Christ (Colossians 2:3). Any system of thought such as evolution or big bang is inherently irrational because knowledge is not based in Christ. Only evolutionary thinking would lead us to conclude that Adam and his descendants could not write. Early man was very intelligent: Cain built a city (Genesis 4:17), six generations later people were making musical instruments and had figured out how to mine ores and make metals (Genesis 4:21-22), Noah built a huge boat for his family and thousands of animals to survive a year-long flood.

"The fossil record does not prove evolution. Instead, it demonstrates mass destruction on a global scale. In Genesis 6-8 we are told about Noah's Flood, an event that killed all people and air breathing land animals not on board the ark, ripped up plants and vegetation, and buried much of the remains in and under layers that became sedimentary rock. In those layers of rock, we find the fossilized remains of those animal buried in the Flood. We also find the remains of massive amounts of vegetation. This is the likely source of the coal, natural gas, and oil deposits that we use to heat our homes and power our automobiles today. If evolution were true then there should be billions of transitional fossils indicating incremental changes between kinds." (Ken Ham-How do we know the Bible is True?). This lack of evidence puts a huge flaw in Darwin's Theory. I strongly suggest you look at the book of Genesis. God stated ten times that everything was created "after its kind: and would only reproduce "after its kind." The molecules to man theory would not, could not, and will never happen. This makes evolution impossible. Why do we continue to teach our children about evolution. You shouldn't be surprised when children start acting like animals when we tell them they are from animals. There is an increase in school violence, lawlessness, homosexual behavior, pornography, abortion, and many other destructive behaviors.

All of us hold presuppositions impacting the way we see the world around us. Our presuppositions are sometimes hidden in a way that makes them hard to uncover and recognize. Most scientist begin with a presupposition and fail to consider any answer that is not strictly physical, material, or natural. Most scientist will refuse to consider a supernatural explanation. Science is skewed to ignore any supernatural explanations. Christians are often accused of being biased simply because they believe in the supernatural. If evidence pointed to the existence of God this would open the possibility of miracles. If God exists than he is the creator of everything we see in the universe. He created matter from nonmatter, life from nonlife, he created all time and space. God's creation of the universe would be miraculous. What we observe in the world confirms what we read in Scripture: organisms reproduce according to their kind as discussed in Genesis 1:24; fossils and rock layers are the watery graveyard from the flood of Noah's day; and genetics shows we're all one race as the Bible teaches in Acts 17:26.

The universe is logical and orderly. "Science requires uniformity. Uniformity requires a biblical worldview. Therefore, science requires a biblical worldview." (Ken Ham-How do we know the Bible is true?). Only a God who is beyond time, consistent, faithful, all powerful, omnipresent, and who has revealed Himself to mankind can guarantee that there will be uniformity throughout space and time. "Evolution is anti-science and anti-knowledge. If evolution were true, science would not be possible because there would be no reason to accept the uniformity of nature upon which all science and technology depend. Nor would there be any reason to think that rational analysis would be possible science the thoughts of our mind would be nothing more than the inevitable result of mindless chemical reactions. Evolutionist are able to do science and gain knowledge only because they are inconsistent; professing to believe in evolution while accepting the principles of biblical creation." (Ken Ham-How do we know the Bible is true?).

Creation cannot be scientifically proven. "Dr. Henry Morris III stated, the central message (of the Bible) cannot be tested in a laboratory by scientific analysis or verified by archeological research. The foundation of truth begins in Genesis." (Ken Ham-How do we know the Bible is true?). It takes faith, but this faith is not blind.

Archaeology-

Many times archaeologists have mocked at people, events, or places mentioned in the Bible only to find evidence of these same people, events, or places later. For example, Isaiah 20:1 mentions an Assyrian King named Sargon. No such king was found on Assyrian king lists so archaeologists and historians assumed the Bible was wrong. Until they discovered his palace and an inscription endorsing the very battle mentioned by Isaiah!! Archaeology continues to corroborate the gospels. Pontius Pilate is the governor of Judea who authorized the crucifixion of Jesus. "In 1961, a piece of limestone was discovered bearing an inscription with Pilate's name. The inscription was discovered in Casarea, a provincial capital during Pilates term (AD 26-36), and it describes a building dedication from Pilate to Tiberius Caser. This single discovery corroborates what the gospel writers said about Pilate existence in history, his position within the government, and his relationship to Tiberius Casar." (Wallace-Cold Case Christianity). Other biblical characters in the Bible are corroborated by archaeology they are the following: Caiaphas-a high priest who presided over the trial of Jesus, Serguius Paulus discussed in Acts 13, Lysanias discussed in Luke Chapter 3, Gallio discussed in Acts 18:12-17, Erastus is discussed in Romans Chapter 16:23, Quirinius was a Syrian governor who was conducting a census when Joseph and Mary returned to Bethlehem. (Wallace-Cold Case Christianity). Archaeology can confirm these people existed and their titles. The book Cold-Case Christianity by Warner Wallace gives a detailed description of the Archaeological finding of each person.

New Testament cities and Locations are corroborated by Archaeology. These places are the following: Bethlehem, Nazareth, Capernaum, Bethsaida, Iconium, The pool of Bethesda, the pool of Siloam, and the Tomb of Lazarus. The book Cold-Case Christianity by Warner Wallace gives a detailed description of the Archaeological finding of each location.

New Testament customs, events, and conditions are corroborated by archaeology. They are the following: The custom of Crucifixion, the existence of synagogues, the behavior of government, the nature of fishing boats, the prevalence of leprosy. The book Cold-Case Christianity by Warner Wallace gives a detailed description of the Archaeological finding of these.

While archaeology can never "prove the Bible true" in that the Bibles most important message is about God's promise of the Savior Jesus Christ, the accuracy of its historical data confirms the integrity of its message.

Eye witness Accounts-

The eyewitnesses were conscientious and protective. The writers of Scripture identify themselves as eyewitnesses and viewed their writings as testimony. Peter called himself a "witness of Christ's sufferings" (1 Peter 5:1 NIV) and one of many "eyewitnesses of his majesty" (2 Peter.1:16-17 NIV). The apostle John claimed he was writing as an eyewitness when he described the life and death of Jesus. He identified himself as "the disciple who testifies to these things and who wrote them down" (John 21:24 NIV), and said he was reporting that "which we have heard, which we have seen with our eyes, which we have looked at and our hands have touched" (1John 1:1 NIV). The apostles saw themselves first and foremost as a group of eyewitnesses, and they understood their shared observations were a powerful testimony to what they claimed to be true. When Judas left the group, they quickly replaced him and demonstrated the high value they placed on their status as eyewitnesses. They set out to "choose one of the men who have been with us the whole time the Lord Jesus was living among us, beginning from John's baptism to the time when Jesus was taken up from us" (Acts 1:21-22 NIV). They replaced Judas with another eyewitness. If you read Acts, you will see the apostles repeatedly identified themselves as eyewitnesses and called upon their testimony as the foundation for all their preaching and teaching. In Peter's very first sermon at Pentecost, he told the crowd the disciples "are all witnesses of it" of the resurrections (Acts 2:32 NIV), and he repeated this claim later at Solomon's Colonnade (Acts 3:15). When Peter and John were eventually arrested for testifying about the resurrection, they told the members of the Sanhedrin "we cannot help speaking about what we have seen and heard" (Acts 4:20 NIV), and they promptly returned to the streets where they "continued to testify to the resurrection of the Lord Jesus" (Acts 4:33 NIV). The apostles clearly and repeatedly identified themselves as "witnesses of all he (Jesus) did throughout Judea and in Jerusalem" (Acts 10:39 NLT) and used this status as the foundation for everything they taught. Even Paul relied on his status as an eyewitness. When Christian communities began to blossom across Asia Minor, Paul wrote to many of them and identified himself as both an apostle and as someone who could testify as an eyewitness. Paul said Jesus "appeared to James, then to all the apostles, and last of all he appeared to me also" (1Cor. 15:7-8 NIV).

The authors of the Gospels were not "Christian" believers until after they observed the life and ministry of Jesus. The Gospels are filled with examples of the disciples' misunderstandings the predictions and proclamations of Jesus. The skeptical disciples continually asked Jesus for clarifications and Thomas after spending 3 years with Jesus still wouldn't believe his predictions of the resurrection until he saw Jesus with his own eyes and touched Jesus with his own hands. The apostles became convinced of Jesus's deity AFTER they observed his life and resurrection. Not a single disciple recanted their claims related to the resurrections. NOT ONE. To take it a step further the 120 disciples in the upper room (Acts 1:15) also did not recant their statement. To take it even further the five hundred eyewitnesses described by Paul (1 Cor. 15:6) also did not recant their statement. These eyewitnesses even in the face of gruesome death and prison never recanted their statement. Andrew was crucified in Patras, Greece. Bartholomew (Nathanael) was flayed to death with a whip in Armenia. James the just was thrown from the temple and then beaten to death in Jerusalem. James the Greater was beheaded in Jerusalem. John died in exile at the prison mines on the island of Patmos. Luke was hanged in Greece. Mark was dragged by horse until he died in Alexandria, Egypt. Matthew was killed by a sword in Ethiopia. Matthias was stoned and then beheaded in Jerusalem. Peter was crucified upside down in Rome. Philip was crucified in Phrygia. Thomas was stabbed to death with a spear in India. History is filled with examples of men and women who were committed to their religious views and were willing to die for what they believed.

There are many nonbiblical eyewitnesses who have corroborated the Gospels. Ancient observers and writers who were hostile to Christianity reluctantly admitted several key facts on the claims of the Christian eyewitnesses, even though they denied Jesus was who he claimed to be. Here are just a few: Josephus (Ad 37-101), Thallus (CA. AD 5-60), Tacitus (AD 56-117) Mara Bar-Serapion (AD 70 UNK.), Phlegon (AD 80-140). The details on how these ancient observers corroborated the Gospels can be found in the book Cold-Case Christianity By J. Warner Wallace. Their statements are astonishing.

The Jewish authorities took many precautions to make sure Jesus' tomb was guarded and sealed, knowing the removal of the body would allow the disciples to claim Jesus had risen see Matt

27:62-66. As many as five hundred people were available to testify to their observations of the risen Christ (according to Paul in 1 Cor. 15:3-8). Jesus had a high regard for evidence. In John 14:11, He told those watching him to examine the evidence of the miracles. If they did not believe what he said about his identity. Even after the resurrection, Jesus stayed with his disciples for an additional forty days and provided them with many convincing proofs. Jesus understood the role and value of evidence and the importance of developing an evidential faith. The evidence supports the act the gospel writes were present in the first century, and their claims are consistent with many pieces of corroborative evidence. Their testimony appears early enough in history, and their claims can be corroborated.

Theology-

The Bible was written over a period of 1600 years by over 40 human authors and yet it is utterly consistent in its message. If the Bible were cobbled together over such a long time by so many people and without an ultimate Author, we'd expect inconsistencies, mistakes, and major changes of theme. But we don't find that. Instead, we have a book that doesn't contradict itself, contains no mistakes, and has consistent theme which is the redemption of sinful man by the holy Creator God. The conclusion that Jesus was resurrected as reported in the Gospels can be inferred from the available evidence. Jesus died and was buried, the tomb was empty, the disciples claimed to see Jesus resurrected, the disciples were transformed. The resurrection is reasonable.

The copyists and scribes were meticulous. The ancient Jewish religious culture was already well established in the first century, and it was from this culture the apostles and first believers emerged. There were priests (Deut. 31:24-26) and scribes called sopherim who were given the responsibility of copying and meticulously caring for the sacred text. The scribes continued to work in Jesus's day and were mentioned throughout the New Testament by the eyewitness who observed them along the Pharisees and other Jewish religious leaders. The Old Testament Scriptures were protected during this period because they considered them the holy Word of God. It's clear the Jews guarded Scripture with extreme care and precision. It's reasonable to conclude the New Testament documents were handled and preserved like other cherished, ancient Scripture.

William Tyndal lived in the early 16th century when only certain people were allowed to interpret the Bible, which was only available in Latin, not the language of the common man. He sought to bring God's Word to the average person by translating it into English. This allowed even children to learn about God and have a personal relationship with him. The Bible is written in such a way that a child can understand the basic message, and yet the most educated theologians continue to learn new things from the Bible as they study it.

"The oldest complete, surviving copy of the New Testament we have (Codex Sinaiticus) was discovered in the Monastery of Saint Catherine, Mount Sinai. Constatine Tischendorf observed it and published the discovery in the nineteenth century; scholars believe it was produced sometime close to AD 350. The text of Codex Sinaiticus provides us with a picture of what the New Testament said in the fourth century, and scholars have used it to inform and confirm the content of Bible translations for many years now." (Wallace-Cold Case Christianity). The apostle John (ca. AD 35-117) was the youngest of Jesus's disciples. John's students confirmed the accuracy of the Gospels. John taught Ignatius. Ignatius wrote letters from AD 105 to AD 115 these letters confirm New Testament concepts. John also taught Polycarp. The content of Polycarp's letter (an ancient document written from AD 100-150 and well attested in history) refers to Ignatius personally and is completely consistent with the content of Ignatius's letters. Ignatius and Polycarp taught Irenaeus who served as a bishop. Irenaeus taught Hippolytus who was said to be a courageous man. The apostle Paul (ca AD 5-67) also had students who confirmed the accuracy of the Gospels. Paul taught Linus and Clement of Rome. Linus is specifically mentioned in 2 Timothy 4:21 as a coworker. Clement is also a co worker mentioned in Philippines 4:3. Clement passed the truth from Evaristus to

Pius 1. These men understood the importance of guarding these accounts for future generations. Pius 1 and Justin Martyr guarded the accounts. Justing was raised Pagan, called himself a Samaritan, studied philosophy and eventually converted to Christianity. Justing taught Tatian. The apostle Peter (ca. 1 BC-AD67 was probable the oldest of Jesus's disciples. Peter communicated through Mark. Mark taught Anianus, Avilius, Kedron, Primus, and Justus. Justus passed the truth to Pantaenus. Pantaenus had students and those students had students. Each one of these students gives a detailed account of the disciples, Jesus, and the New Testament.

"From the earliest nonbiblical records, we would learn the following: Jesus was predicted by the Old Testament prophets. He was a man in the line of David, conceived by the Holy Spirit as the only begotten Son of God, born of the virgin Mary. And announced with a star. He came forth from God and manifested God's will and knowledge. He was baptized by John the Baptists, lived a humble, unassuming, perfect, and sinless life, spoke the words of God and taught people many important divine truths (including the principles we recognize from the Sermon on the Mount). Although Jesus was anointed with oil, He was unjustly treated and condemned, whipped, and ultimately executed on the cross. This execution took place during the government of Pontius Pilate and the reign of Herod the Tetrarch. Jesus's death was a personal sacrifice. He offered to Do on our behalf as a payment for the debt of our sin. Jesus proved his divinity by physically resurrecting from the dead, appearing to Peter and the other disciples, eating with them, and encouraging them to touch Him and see for themselves. Emboldened by their observations of the risen Jesus, the disciples were fearless. They understood their eternal life and resurrection were assured based on their faith in Jesus, who now reigned in heaven and lived in everyone who accepted His offer of forgiveness and salvation. Jesus was (and Is) the 'Door,' the 'Bread of Life,' the Eternal Word,' the 'Son of God,' our 'High Priests,' 'Savior,' 'Master,' 'Guardian,' 'Helper,' 'Refuge,' and 'Lord.' Jesus and the Father are one; Jesus possesses eternal glory and majesty. All creation belongs to Him and is subject to Him. Jesus will judge the living and the dead. Jesus Is 'God.' We would learn all this, not based on the gospel accounts, but based on what is described by the earliest first-century students of the gospel writers. Specifically, Ignatius, Polycarp, and Clement confirm the accuracy of the Gospels. This version of Jesus was witnessed and accurately described by the gospel writers and confirmed by their students. The earliest accounts of Jesus's story (as given by the eyewitnesses and their students in the first century) is aligned with the version we have 2000 years later." (Wallace-Cold Case Christianity)

If God does exist, why would he allow evil things to happen? "People who complain about evil behavior must accept the premise that true objective right and wrong exists in the first place. They must accept some things are morally virtuous and some things are morally repulsive, no matter who you are, where you are located, or when you live in history. There must be a true barometer of right and wrong. For an act to be objectively bad, there must be some standard of objective good by which to measure it. What might that standard be If not God? Can the standard come from some evolutionary process? Can it come from the slow development of cultural groups? If so, morals are simply a matter of opinion. Remember, even the most heinous regimes of history identified their own behavior as morally virtuous. For true evil to exist, there must be a source of true good transcending all groups who might make a claim about the existence of evil. In other words, the existence of true evil necessitates the presence of God a standard of true virtue. It turns out the existence of evil is another evidence for Gods' existence; another piece of the puzzle revealing God's image." (Wallace-Cold Case Christianity). True love requires humans to freely choose, God's love cannot be forced. It is to be heartfelt and real. People who have the freedom to love often choose to hate. A world in where people have the freedom to love and do great acts of kindness is also a world in where people have the freedom to hate and commit great acts of evil. You cannot have one without the other.

Prophesies- The Old Testament prophesied this Savior would:

- be a descendant of Abraham (Genesis 12:1–3, 22:18)
- be born into the tribe of Judah (Genesis 49:10)
- be born into the lineage of David (2 Samuel 7:12f)
- be born in Bethlehem (Micah 5:2)
- be born to a virgin (Isaiah 7:14)
- come while the temple was still standing (Malachi 3:1)
- open the eyes of the blind, unstop the ears of the deaf, and cause the lame to walk (Isaiah 35:5–6)
- be "despised and rejected" by His own people (Isaiah 53:3; Psalm 118:22; 1 Peter 2:7)

The Scriptures also foretold the precise time in history when He would die (Daniel 9:24–26), how He would die (Psalm 22:16–18; Isaiah 53; Zechariah 12:10), and that He would rise from the dead (Psalm 16:10; Isaiah 53:10–12; Acts 2:27–32). These are just a few of the prophecies that were fulfilled in Jesus' life. The Old Testament, completed 400 years before Jesus' birth, contains more than 300 references to the Messiah that were fulfilled in Jesus' life. And there are hundreds of other prophecies in the Bible that have been fulfilled concerning the rise and fall of nations and other matters. The fulfillment of these prophecies is compelling evidence that these men spoke with the aid of the all-knowing, all-powerful God written about in the Bible—the God who declared: Isaiah 46:9–10 NKJV"I am God, and there is none like Me, declaring the end from the beginning, and from ancient times things that are not yet done."

"Religious books, such as Islam's Koran, Mormonism's Book of

Mormon, and Hinduisms' Veds, Jehovah's Witnesses' watchtower publications, and so on contradict the Bible; and so, they cannot be scripture. For example, the Koran in two chapters (Sura 4:171 and 23:91) says God had no son, but the Bible is clear that Jesus is the only begotten Son of God (Matthew 26:63-64). The Book of Mormon says in Moroni 8:8 that children are not sinners, but the Bible teaches that children are sinful, even from birth (Psalm 51:5). Few would dispute that the Vedas and other writing in Hinduism are starkly different form the Bible. Jehovah's Witness literature has Jesus created, Whereas Jesus is the creator according to John 1, Colossians 1, and Hebrews 1." (Ken Ham-How do we know the Bible is True?). Since these alleged holy books are not from the perfect God, who are they from? They are from imperfect man. The Bible warns that false philosophies will be used to turn people from the Bible (Colossians 2:8). So, people need to stand firm on the Bible and not be swayed (1 Corinthians 15: 58; 2 Thessalonians 2:15). You could either place your faith on the perfect, all-knowing God who has always been there, or trust in the imperfect.

History-

When people understand they can trust the history in the early chapters of Genesis, they can better understand and be more responsive to the gospel. The Bible records the details of the creation of the universe, the origin of life, the moral law of God, the history of man's rebellion against God, and the historical details of God's work of redemption for all who trust in His Son. The Bible also claims to be God's revelation to mankind. This teaches us how we should live, why we exist, what happens when we die, and what our meaning and purpose is. The Old Testament is ruthless in honesty. If Israel lost a battle it was recorded. When Israel's hero King David committed a terrible double crime of adultery and murder, that was also recorded. Historians and archaeologists continually affirm the accuracy of the Bible in matters of history. The number of ancient manuscripts of the Bible far exceeds that of other ancient documents. "Beyond the Bible, we can find information from several other sources. The non-Christian writers Josephus, Lucian, and Tacitus, among others wrote of Christ's Crucifixion and the early days of Christianity." (Ken Ham-How do we know the Bible to be True). The Bible is not just a history book. It is inspired by the almighty God himself. Given that the Bible has demonstrated itself to be the Word of God and God is the source of all knowledge (Colossians 2:30), it is impossible for God to be wrong about anything. The Bibles account of death and resurrection is the most reliable account of evidence.

The first five books of the Bible are written by Moses. How did Moses get information prior to his own life. Moses could have obtained this information through divine revelations, previously written texts passed down through the generations, and/or oral tradition from his ancestors. Regardless, under the guidance of the Holy Spirit (2 Peter 1:20-21), the books of Moses would be completely true and without error. "Take note of some of the references back to Moses' work. For example, John 7:22 and Acts 15:1 refer to Moses giving the doctrine of circumcision. Yet John also reveals that this came earlier-in Genesis, with Abraham. Nevertheless, it is credited to Moses because it was recorded in his writing. The New Testament attributes all the books from Genesis through Deuteronomy as being the writings of Moses. So, to attack the Mosaic authorship of the first five books of the Old Testament then is to attack the truthfulness of the rest of the biblical writers and Jesus Himself." (Ken Ham-How do we Know the Bible is True?) Deuteronomy, the author of the obiturary of Moses was probably Joshua, a close associate of Moses who was chosen by God to lead the people of Israel into the Promised Land (for Moses was not allowed to because of his disobedience), and who was inspired by God to write the next book in the Old Testament. A similar obiturary of Joshua was added by an inspired editor to the end of Joshua's book (Joshua 24: 29-33). "There is abundant biblical and extra-biblical evidence that Moses wrote the first five books of the Bible called the Pentateuch during the wilderness wandering after the Jews left their slavery in Egypt and before they entered the Promised Land (about 1445-1405 B.C.). Contrary to the liberal theologians and other skeptics, it was not written after the Jews returned from exile in Babylon (ca. 500 B.C.)" (Ken Ham-How do we Know the Bible is true?). Christians should believe God rather than the fallible sinful skeptics. As Paul says in Romans 3:4 KJV, "Let God be true but every man a liar." God commanded Moses to place a copy of his writing in the ark of the covenant in the Holy of Holies (Deuteronomy 10:2). After the death of Moses, God gave Israel's new leader, Joshua, special instructions concerning these books.

The New Testament treats Genesis 1-11 as historical narrative. At least 25 New Testament passages refer directly to the early chapters of Genesis, and they are always treated as real history. Genesis 1 and 2 were cited by Jesus in response to a question about divorce (Matthew 19: 4-6; Mark 10: 6-9? Paul referenced Genesis 2-3 in Romans 5:12-19; 1 Corinthians 15: 20-22, 45-47; 2 Corinthians 11:3; and 1 Timothy 2:13-14. The death of Able recorded in Genesis 4 is mentioned by Jesus in Luke 11:51. The Flood (Genesis 6-9) is confirmed as historical by Jesus (Matthew 24:37-39) and Peter (2 Peter 2:4-9, 3:6), and in Luke 17:26-29, Jesus mentioned the flood in the same context as He did the account of Lot and Sodom (Genesis 19). There is geological evidence that is absolutely in harmony with the word of God on the earth's history of the Flood. Finally, in Luke's genealogy of Christ, he includes 20 names found in the genealogies of Genesis 5 and 11 (Luke 3:34-38). When you treat Genesis as a historical narrative it is clear that God created everything in six normal length days approximately 6,000 years ago.

When the Dead Sea Scrolls were discovered in 1947, no one had been aware of their existence for nearly 2,000 years. When those manuscripts were compared to the existing manuscripts the differences were inconsequential.

Laws of Logic-

Human wisdom comes from reason; godly wisdom comes from revelation. Mankind have made some amazing things happen. We have put a man on the moon, made inventions and cured diseases just to name a few. We have much knowledge. But for all this knowledge and achievement, we have yet to discover a source of wisdom on earth that can pull all the pieces of life together. Although men can do all these things they don't know where to find wisdom and understanding. Proverbs 1:7 NIV "The fear of the LORD is the beginning of knowledge." We need to think critically as Christians. We must dig into the Bible to understand God's Word. "The critic asserts that the Bible is false because if contains contradictions. Perhaps the most intriguing aspect of this claim is that it backfires on the critic. The reason is this: If the Bible is true, would contradictions be unacceptable! Most people simply assume the law of non-contradictions; they take it for granted that a contradiction cannot be true. But have you ever stopped to think about why a contradiction cannot be true? Only in a biblical worldview can we know that contradictions are always false, only the Christian has a basis for the law of non-contradictions." (Ken Ham-How do we know the Bible is True?). The Christian can account for laws of logic; they are the correct standard reasoning because God is sovereign over all truth. We can know some of God's thoughts because God has revealed Himself to us through the words of Scripture and the person of Jesus Christ.

"The truth of the Bible is obvious to anyone willing to investigate it. The Bible is uniquely self-consistent and extraordinarily authentic. It has changed the lives of millions of people who have placed their faith in Christ. It has been confirmed countless times by archaeology and other sciences. It possesses divine insight into the nature of the universe and has made correct predictions about distant future events with perfect accuracy. When Christians read the Bible, they cannot help but recognize the voice of their Creator. The Bible claims to be the word of God, and it demonstrates this claim by making knowledge possible. It is the standard of standards. The proof of the Bible is that unless its truth is presupposed, we couldn't prove anything at all." (Ken Ham-How do we know the Bible is true?)

According to Scriptures, the Christian faith is not a "blind faith." It is a faith that is rationally defensible. It is logical and self-consistent. It can make sense of what we experience in the world.

Christians have a moral obligation to think rationally. We are to be imitators of God (Ephesians 5:1), patterning our thinking after His revelations (Isaiah 55:7-8; Psalm 36:9. "There are those who would challenge the rationality of the biblical worldview. Some say that the Christian worldview is illogical on the face of it. After all, the Bible speaks of floating ax heads, the sun apparently going backward, a universe created in six days, an earth that has pillars and corners, people walking on water, light before the sun, a talking serpent, a talking donkey, dragons, and a senior citizen taking two of every land animal on a big boat! The critic suggests that no rational person can possibly believe in such things in our modern age of scientific enlightenment. He claims that to believe in such things would be illogical. The Bible does make some extraordinary claims. But are such claims truly illogical? Do they actually violate any laws of logic? Although the above biblical examples go beyond our ordinary, everyday experiences, none of them are contradictory. They do not violate any laws of logic. Some biblical criticisms involve misuse of language: taking figures of speech (e.g., 'pillars of the earth') as though these were literal, when this is clearly not the case. This is an error on the part of the critic, not an error in the text. Poetic sections of the Bible, such as the psalms, and figures of speech should be taken as such. To do otherwise is academically dishonest." (Ken Ham-The New Answers Book 3). God Himself is the limit of what is possible. His word is therefore the standard of what is reasonable. God is all knowing, all powerful, and beyond time. An all-powerful God can make a donkey talk, can create the universe in six days, can bring two of every animal to Noah, etc. These are simply not problems in the biblical worldview. When the critic dismisses the miraculous solely on the basis that it is miraculous, he is simply begging the question.

"The atheist cannot account for the existence of laws of logic-why they are immaterial, why they are universal, why they do not change with time, and how human beings can possibly know about them or their properties. The biblical God must exist in order for reasoning to be possible. Therefore, the best proof of God's existence is that without Him we couldn't prove anything at all."

(Ken Ham-The New Answers Book 3). The atheist who denies God is an emotional and spiritual reaction not a logical one. As shown in 1 Corinthians 12:3; 2 Timothy 2:25, It is the Holy Spirit that must give the ability to repent. It is not the Christians job to convert people. It is the holy Spirit that brings conversion. Our job is to give a defense of the faith in a way that is faithful to the Scriptures (1 Peter 3:15). God can use our arguments as part of the process by which He draws people to Himself.

The real issue is not about evidence; it is a heart issue. As Christians we are called to have ready answers and break down strongholds that act as stumbling blocks to the unbeliever. It is the Holy Spirit that changes lives. "But sanctify the Lord God in your hearts, and always be ready to give a defense to everyone who asks you a reason for the hope that is in you, with meekness and fear" (1 Peter 3:15 NKJV). "For the weapons of our warfare are not carnal but mighty in God for pulling down strongholds, casting down arguments and every high thing that exalts itself against the knowledge of God, bringing every thought into captivity to the obedience of Christ" (2 Corinthians 10: 4-5 KJV).

LAST THOUGHT ON RELIGION

" **M**ost People Are Religious-Of a worldwide population of 7.5 billion, 80% identify with a religion. Christianity, with 2.1 billion people, is the most practiced religion, followed by Islam, Hinduism, Buddhism, and Sikhism. Of U.S. citizens, 89% say they believe in God, and 70.6% identify as Christian. Benefits of Religion-People who are highly religious—who pray each day and go to services at least once a week—are "more engaged with their extended families, more likely to volunteer, more involved in their communities and generally happier with the way things are going in their lives, Of the highly religious, 65% say they have donated money, time or goods to help the poor in the past week, compared with 41% of people who say they are less religious." (According to Pew Research)

7 Reasons Religion Is Good for You

1. Lower blood pressure. A Duke University Medical Center study found that religious older adults are 40% less likely to have high blood pressure than adults who said they weren't religious.

2. Healthier immune system. Another study found that older adults who regularly attended religious services were about half as likely as those who don't to have high levels of interleukin-6, an inflammatory protein in the immune system linked to certain cancers, autoimmune diseases, and some viral infections.

3. Longer survival with cancer. Religious late-stage cancer patients had a higher (7.4%) rate of resuscitation than those who weren't (1.8%).

4. More satisfaction. Religious people report that they're happier. A study in the American Sociological Review indicates this is likely because regular church attendance leads to strong social bonds within congregations. "We all will eventually move in certain directions in life as a result of all this and the measurement I suggest is the degree of happiness, satisfaction, and fulfillment our particular state in life brings about for us will be equal to the degree to which we have successfully determined God's will for our lives and made it our own," said Father Joe Ferraioli, O.M.I., chaplain at Benedictine Living Community-At The Shrine.

5. Longevity. People who attend religious services live seven years longer compared to those who never go. This is attributed to the social benefits of religion.

6. Protects against depression. Older patients with depressive symptoms recovered better if religion played a large part in their lives.

7. Reduces stress. Periods of respite from daily life lead to a reduction in stress. According to Benedictine Pastoral Care Director Mary Mertzlufft, "When we center ourselves through being quiet in God's presence within us, we look at life with different eyes, perhaps giving others an excuse or putting things into a balanced perspective." https://www.benedictineliving.org/blog/7-reasons-religion-is-good-for-you/?utm_term=how%20does%20religion%20benefit%20society&utm_campaign=Wellness+Blog+and+Resources&utm_source=adwords&utm_medium=ppc&hsa_acc=3146124880&hsa_cam=1373743432&hsa_grp=56579487738&hsa_ad=267848176717&hsa_src=g&hsa_tgt=kwd-1443523477589&hsa_kw=how%20does%20religion%20benefit%20society&hsa_mt=b&hsa_net=adwords&hsa_ver=3&gclid=Cj0KCQiAutyfBhCMARIsAMgcRJRPy4GjDQM25IA11MFuMNplYm78d4ZNIqe5Bv7EMmTa0baQohiadq0aAjArEALw_wcB

https://qz.com/1301084/should-you-raise-your-kids-religious-heres-what-the-science-says

CONCLUSION

GRACE WITHOUT TRUTH IS COMPROMISE, AND TRUTH WITHOUT GRACE IS HEARTLESS. I desire to be biblical in my teaching. A true Christian in not ashamed of the gospel and does not bring shame to it. Both the Old and New Testaments uses the word meaning "peculiar" (Exodus 19:5; 1 Peter 2:9) to describe the role of God's people-a word that means "unique in character and value." This uniqueness means turning away from political and spiritual corruption, injustice, violence, treachery, gluttony, idolatry. I see myself as a peculiar witness to the world. I know I'm not alone. The peculiar power that I have is the Holy Spirit. Preaching the word of God is not always easy. The message we are required to proclaim is often offensive. We are not to water down or trim or tailor the message to people's preference. If we are not sharing the gospel with others, then we have not heard it ourselves. "All scripture is given by inspiration of God, and is profitable doctrine, for reproof, for correction, for instruction in righteousness" (2 Timothy 3:16 NKJV). This is the Word to be preached: the whole counsel of God (Acts 20:27). Not only are we to preach the Word, we must do it regardless of the climate of opinion around us. We are commanded to be faithful when such preaching is tolerated-but also when it is not. In the Bible Paul urges Timothy to be willing to suffer for the truth's sake, and keep preaching the Word faithfully. 2 Timothy 4:4 NIV says people will ultimately "turn their ears from the truth, and turn aside to myths." They become the victims of their own refusal to hear the truth. As soon as they turn away from the truth, they become pawns of Satan. "For some Christians, their first encounter with atheistic opposition occurs at the university level, either as a student or the parent of a student. The number of young Christians who reject Christianity in college is alarming, according to nearly every study done on the topic. Part of this is a matter of preparation. We need to master the facts and evidence supporting the claims of Christianity and anticipate the tactics of those who oppose us." (Wallace- Cold Case Christianity). This kind of preparation is a form of worship. When we devote ourselves to this rational preparation and study, we are worshipping God with our mind, the very thing he has called us to do (Matt. 22:37). If you are in Christ, and Christ is in you, then the world should see nothing else. The more I learn about the world in which we live, the clearer it becomes that there must be a divine Planner. I had a calling from God to write. God told me to write and I wrote. I set aside an hour a day to dedicate myself to this paper for four years. God gives me ideas to write about, books to read, as well as me jotting down my own experiences. I give full credit to my Lord and Savior for giving me the desire and dedication to write this. Everything I do I commit it to the Lord. God will always reveal his will to the one who is willing to do it. God's will is plain to those who will look for it. Are you willing to follow the plan God has for you? Have you committed your dreams and ambitions to God? He may want to approve and confirm them; or he may want to change and refashion them into something you've never dreamed of. Henry Ford once said "Anyone who stops learning is old, whether at twenty or eighty. Anyone who keeps learning stays young." God has something for you to learn. According to Ephesians 4:12, God gives us special abilities to do certain things best, so that God's people will be equipped to do better work for him building up the Church, the body of Christ, to a position of strength.

It is one thing to have convictions; it is something else again to be convicted for your convictions! There are so many stories of men and woman in the Bible and even today that took their faith so seriously that they were imprisoned and martyred for what they believed. As a Christian college professor, I wanted to express my legal way of Academic Freedom and what better way to do that then to write this book. I do feel as though I have been discriminated in the work place due to my religious beliefs. Our Religion greatly affects our children's development from everything to child rearing, parenting styles, academics, our health, and marriages. Religion should be talked about often in a child development class. Religion is talked about in various child development textbooks. Moreover, a religious upbringing also contributes to several positive outcomes, such as greater happiness, more volunteering in the community, a greater sense of mission and purpose, and higher levels of forgiveness. Christianity has made an impact on society and culture through colleges, science, music, art, books, movies and tv shows. Every aspect of our life has been impacted by a Christian in history. My son told me how his science teacher in high school talked about new earth Vs. old earth and that Religion is often talked about in his High School history class often mentioning Jesus Christ, the Roman Empire, and Julius Caeser. So what is the BIG deal if I mention religion or faith that is BASED ON WHAT IS ALREADY IN OUR CURRICULM. As I mentioned before I'm only addressing what is already in our child development textbook and really does only take a few minutes of class time. I pose discussion questions and the students discuss. There are meaningful though provoking questions and answers by students. Of course, Student learning outcomes are being met. Students are never graded on anything religious based and I do not feel as though I am forcing my faith on students. I have never had a formal complaint against a student and feel as though my teachings are justified. Although I am a senior adjunct, a year has passed and I have been given no classes. A punishment from the college basically saying fall in line with the indoctrination of our college or we will not give you any classes. The saying goes "Go Woke or Go Broke" comes to mind. I was bitter and filled with grief for a job that I loved so much to be taken from me, but then I came across Genesis 50:20 NIV, "You intended to harm me, but God intended it for good to accomplish what is now being done, the saving of many lives." Unexpected blessings are wonderful. Unexpected trials are often bitter pills to swallow. But God can use even unexpected trials to bring unexpected blessings. I never would have written this book had I not of had that job. What happened at that job had to happen for me to write this book. Just because God has promised to fight for you does not mean you can sit idly by and do nothing. I had to act. I wanted to quit, call in sick, but then I thought about how Jesus faced conflict he didn't run from it. I see how I was able to learn from my trials more than my triumphs. God shaped me into a vessel for greater service. Standing your ground is easier when you're grounded in faith. Can you stand your ground when you are in the minority? How about when the minority is shrinking and the opposition is growing? God is my problem solver and he is my shield to protect me. God gives me peace even in the most difficult moments and fearlessness in the face of opposition. Truly without God there is no victory and with God every rival can be vanquished. I will not be feared into silence, even in the face of fear I am someone who's not going to back down from doing what I feel to be right, fair, and moral. Events that have been surprising to me are opportunities for surrendering to God. I think of David in the Bible even though he was under enemy attack, during fearful circumstances, when words and thoughts are turned against him, when tears flow in the solitude of his suffering-through it all, God is with him and for him (Psalms 56:9). In the midst of what I felt like was Christian persecution in the work place I stood strong and bold in my faith and the words Trust in the Lord for he is for you, and Psalm 13 gave me hope. A Christian should never let hardship get him down except down on his knees to pray. When a storm is coming ships need strong anchors, buildings need a strong foundation, and trees need a deep root system. To survive the storm their needs to be a strong link to something unmovable. My anchor in a stormy circumstance was an unshakable faith, in an unchanging God. I stayed focused on my link of faith to God. It is easy to complain about the enemies around you, but I learned from David's story that we can praise God for those circumstances and respond with a joyful attitude of praise-which at times is hard to do. Your enemies will either drive you from God or cause you to walk closer to God. God's justice shows that the joy of the wicked is short-lived. We become what we worship. Do you worship man or God? Do you worship what society says is morally good or do your morals align with biblical truth? Do you worship your home, entertainment, cell phone, money, or your job? I can see how my enemies don't worship God just as David's enemies didn't. God is looking for those who will exercise truth and love in their daily affairs. What are you willing to give up to put Christ first? Christ is not valued at all unless he is valued above all. Discipleship is costly. It means rearranging priorities, inconveniences, expenses, and personal sacrifice. God develops spiritual power in your life through difficulties. Storms make for strong Christians. Writing this book was daring for me to do regardless of the consequences. Spreading the gospel is not a spare time activity. Worship is not simply a part of the Christian life it IS the Christian life. Thank you, God, for closing doors and opening the doors of opportunities for me. I am ready to see where you take me.

"Only fools say in their hearts 'There is no God.' They are corrupt, and their actions are evil; not one of them does good!" (Psalms 53:1 NLV). Only a fool would try to make it on his own merits when the way has already been provided by God. Are you putting off accepting Jesus Christ as your Savior, or keeping an area of your life from God? God is patient because he is eternal. Receive Christ your Savior and Lord. Believe that Jesus lived, died, and rose again in payment for your sin (John 3:16, Romans 10:9). Jesus says, "I am the door. If anyone enters by Me, he will be saved" (John 10:9 NKJV). Rely on God's strength. God does not promise that life as a Christian will be easy or that you will be healthy and wealthy. In fact, you can expect trials in life that will test your faith (James 1:2-3; I Peter 1:6-9). However, God promises that He will give you the strength to bear those burdens (1 Corinthians 10:13). Jesus told His followers in Luke 14:25-33 that they should count the cost before following Him. If this is what you really want, and or desire is to make Him the center of your life, you can receive the Creator's gift (eternal life through faith in Jesus Christ) right now. We cannot rely on God's promises without obeying his commandments. The Bible tells us:

For with the heart, one believes unto righteousness, and with the mouth confession is made unto salvation.... For "whoever calls on the name of the Lord shall be saved" (Romans 10:10-13 NKJV).

You can go to God in prayer right now, right where you are and ask Him for this gift. Here is a suggested prayer to help you:

Lord Jesus, I know that I am a sinner and do not deserve eternal life, but I believe You died for me and rose from the grave to pay the price for my sin. Please forgive me of my sins and save me. I repent of my sins and now place my trust in You for eternal life. I receive the free gift of eternal life. Amen.

Look at what Jesus promises to those who believe in Him: "Most assuredly, I say to you, he who believes in Me has everlasting life" (John 6:47 NKJV). And, "But as many as received Him, to them He gave the right to become children of God, to those who believe in His name" (John 1:12 NKJV).

Will your name be written in the book of life?

CLOSING PRAYER

"In the morning, Lord, you hear my voice; in the morning I lay my requests before You and wait expectantly. For you are not a God who is pleased with wickedness; with You, evil people are not welcome. The arrogant cannot stand in your presence. You hate all who do wrong; you destroy those who tell lies. The bloodthirsty and deceitful you, Lord, detest. But I, by Your great love, can come into Your house; in reverence I bow down toward your holy temple. Lead me, Lord, in your righteousness because of my enemies-make Your way straight before me. Not a word from their mouth can be trusted; their heart is filled with malice. Their throat is an open grave; with their tongues they tell lies. Declare them guilty, o God! Let their intrigues be their downfall. Banish them for their many sins, for they have rebelled against you. But let all who take refuge in You be glad; let them ever sing for joy. Spread Your protection over them, that those who love Your name may rejoice in You." (Psalm 5: 3-11. David NIV)

REFERENCES

1. Berger, Kathleen. (2021). The Developing Person Through Childhood and Adolescence 12th Edition. Worth Publishers, New York.
2. Crosson-Tower, Cynthia. Understanding Child Abuse and Neglect 9th edition
3. Steven Andrew Jacobs. (Fall 2021). The Scientific Consensus on When a Human's Life Begins. Issues Law Med.
4. Berns, Robert M. (2016). Child, Family, School, Community Socialization and Support 10th Edition. Cengage Learning, Stamford, Ct.
5. U.S Census Bureau. (2023). Living arrangements of children under 18 years old: 1960 to present. Washington D.C.:Census Bureau.
6. https://www.cdc.gov Center for Disease Control and Prevention, childhood obesity facts
7. Mena, Janet; Child, Family, and Community Family-Centered Early Care and Education seventh edition; 2017 Pearson
8. Ham, Ken and Ware, Charles. (2017). One Race One Blood. Master Books, New Leaf Publishing Group, www.masterbooks.com
9. Ham, Ken. (2018). One Blood for Kids What the Bible says About Race. Master Books, New Leaf Publishing Group, www.masterbooks.com
10. Azzollini, Meena. (February 8, 2019) How religion impacts development in young children
11. R.L. Hotz. (February 20, 1997). Race has no basis in biology, researchers say, Cincinnati Enquirer, p. A3.
12. Ham, Ken. (August 12, 2020) New to Homeschooling

13. (Social Psychological and Personality Science).

14. Thomas Jefferson, Jefferson's Letter to the Danbury Baptists, The Library of Congress website.

15. Neil A. Campbell, Brad Williamson, and Robin J. Heyden, Biology: Exploring Life, Florida Teacher's Edition (Upper Saddle River, New Jersey: Pearson Prentice Hall, 2006), p. 38.

16. https://youtu.be/mITCu7eRlxE

17. http://www.pbs.org/wgbh/globalconnections/mideast/themes/culture/#:~:text=Religion%20in%20the%20cultures%20of%20the%20Middle%20East&text=Each%20religion%20used%20the%20texts,a%20foundation%20for%20civil%20law.

18. https://www.humanium.org/en/children-and-religions/

19. https://www.mdpi.com/2077-1444/10/11/631

20. https://www.researchgate.net/publication/257656700_Child_Development_from_the_Perspective_of_Syed_Shakh_Ahmad_Alhady

21. https://www.benedictineliving.org/blog/7-reasons-religion-is-good-for-you/?utm_term=how%20does%20religion%20benefit%20society&utm_campaign=Wellness+Blog+and+Resources&utm_source=adwords&utm_medium=ppc&hsa_acc=3146124880&hsa_cam=1373743432&hsa_grp=56579487738&hsa_ad=267848176717&hsa_src=g&hsa_tgt=kwd-1443523477589&hsa_kw=how%20does%20religion%20benefit%20society&hsa_mt=b&hsa_net=adwords&hsa_ver=3&gclid=Cj0KCQiAutyfBhCMARIsAMgcRJRPy4GjDQM25IA11MFuMNplYm78d4ZNIqe5Bv7EMmTa0baQohiadq0aAjArEALw_wcB

22. https://qz.com/1301084/should-you-raise-your-kids-religious-heres-what-the-science-says

23. J. Warner Wallace. (2021). Person of Interest. Published by Zondervan

24. CJ Pearson, (Jan 2, 2023). Why I'm leaving college and choosing education over indoctrination. New York Post.

25. J. Warner Wallace. (2023). Cold-Case Christianity updated and expanded edition. Published by David C Cook.

26. Shapiro, Ben (2004). Brainwashed: How Universities Indoctrinate America's Youth. Published in Nashville, Tennessee, by Thomas Nelson.

27. Ham, Ken. (2021). How do we know the Bible is True? Published Master Books, New Leaf Publishing Group, www.masterbooks.com.

28. Ham, Ken. (2006). The New Answers Book 1 Creation/Evolution and the Bible. Master Books New Leaf Publishing Group, Inc. www.masterbooks.com

29. Ham, Ken. (2008). The New Answers Book 2 creation/evolution and the Bible. Master Books New Leaf Publishing Group, Inc. www.masterbooks.com

30. Ham, Ken. (2010). The New Answers Book 3 creation/evolution and the Bible. Master Books New Leaf Publishing Group, Inc. www.masterbooks.com

31. Ham, Ken. (2013). The New Answers Book 4 creation/evolution and the Bible. Master Books New Leaf Publishing Group, Inc. www.masterbooks.com

32. Mulvihill, Josh. (February 10, 2021) Understanding Educational Equity: What it is and why it should be rejected. Gospel Shaped Family.

33. Holy Bible-God's holy word

Printed in the United States
by Baker & Taylor Publisher Services